The Hedgehog and the Fox

An essay on

Tolstoy's view of history

by Isaiah Berlin

A CLARION BOOK

Published by Simon and Schuster

A CLARION BOOK
PUBLISHED BY SIMON AND SCHUSTER
ROCKEFELLER CENTER, 630 FIFTH AVENUE
NEW YORK, NEW YORK 10020

FIRST CLARION PRINTING 1970

SBN 671-20709-1
MANUFACTURED IN THE UNITED STATES OF AMERICA

To the memory of Jasper Ridley

AUTHOR'S NOTE

MY THANKS are due to Professor S. Konovalov and the Clarendon Press for permission to reproduce the portions of this essay which originally appeared in 1951 under a somewhat different title in the second volume of *Oxford Slavonic Papers*. I have considerably revised the original version, and added two further sections (vi and vii). I should like to thank Mr. Richard Wollheim for reading the new sections and suggesting improvements, and to Mr. J. S. G. Simmons for supplying me with a valuable reference and for his care in seeing the earlier version through the press.

I. B.

Oxford, July 1953

THE HEDGEHOG AND THE FOX

'A queer combination of the brain of an English chemist
with the soul of an Indian Buddhist.'   E. M. DE VOGÜÉ

I

THERE is a line among the fragments of the Greek
poet Archilochus which says: 'The fox knows many
things, but the hedgehog knows one big thing'.[1]
Scholars have differed about the correct interpretation of these dark words, which may mean no more
than that the fox, for all his cunning, is defeated by
the hedgehog's one defence. But, taken figuratively,
the words can be made to yield a sense in which they
mark one of the deepest differences which divide
writers and thinkers, and, it may be, human beings in
general. For there exists a great chasm between
those, on one side, who relate everything to a single
central vision, one system less or more coherent or
articulate, in terms of which they understand, think
and feel—a single, universal, organizing principle in
terms of which alone all that they are and say has
significance—and, on the other side, those who pursue
many ends, often unrelated and even contradictory,
connected, if at all, only in some *de facto* way, for some
psychological or physiological cause, related by no
moral or aesthetic principle; these last lead lives,
perform acts, and entertain ideas that are centrifugal
rather than centripetal, their thought is scattered or
diffused, moving on many levels, seizing upon the
essence of a vast variety of experiences and objects for
what they are in themselves, without, consciously or
unconsciously, seeking to fit them into, or exclude
them from, any one unchanging, all-embracing,

[1] Πόλλ’ οἶδ’ ἀλώπηξ ἀλλ’ ἐχῖνος ἓν μέγα. (Diehl, *Frag.* 103.)

sometimes self-contradictory and incomplete, at times fanatical, unitary inner vision. The first kind of intellectual and artistic personality belongs to the hedgehogs, the second to the foxes; and without insisting on a rigid classification, we may, without too much fear of contradiction, say that, in this sense, Dante belongs to the first category, Shakespeare to the second; Plato, Lucretius, Pascal, Hegel, Dostoevsky, Nietzsche, Ibsen, Proust are, in varying degrees, hedgehogs; Herodotus, Aristotle, Montaigne, Erasmus, Molière, Goethe, Pushkin, Balzac, Joyce are foxes.

Of course, like all over-simple classifications of this type, the dichotomy becomes, if pressed, artificial, scholastic, and ultimately absurd. But if it is not an aid to serious criticism, neither should it be rejected as being merely superficial or frivolous; like all distinctions which embody any degree of truth, it offers a point of view from which to look and compare, a starting-point for genuine investigation. Thus we have no doubt about the violence of the contrast between Pushkin and Dostoevsky; and Dostoevsky's celebrated speech about Pushkin has, for all its eloquence and depth of feeling, seldom been considered by any perceptive reader to cast light on the genius of Pushkin, but rather on that of Dostoevsky himself, precisely because it perversely represents Pushkin—an arch-fox, the greatest in the nineteenth century—as a being similar to Dostoevsky who is nothing if not a hedgehog; and thereby transforms, indeed distorts, Pushkin into a dedicated prophet, a bearer of a single, universal message which was indeed the centre of Dostoevsky's own universe, but exceedingly remote from the many varied provinces of Pushkin's protean genius. Indeed, it would not be absurd to say that Russian literature is spanned by these gigantic figures—at one pole Pushkin, at the other Dostoevsky; and that the characteristics of other Russian writers can, by those who find it useful or enjoyable to ask that kind of question, to some degree be determined in relation to these great opposites. To ask of Gogol', Turgenev, Chekhov, Blok how they stand in relation to Pushkin and to Dostoevsky leads—or, at any rate, has led—to fruitful and illuminating criticism. But when we come to Count Lev Nikolaevich Tolstoy, and ask this of him—ask whether he belongs to the first category or the second, whether he is a monist or a pluralist, whether his vision is of one or of many, whether he is of a single substance or compounded of heterogeneous elements, there is no clear or immediate answer. The question does not, somehow, seem wholly appropriate; it seems to breed more darkness than it dispels. Yet it is not lack of information that makes us pause: Tolstoy has told us more about himself and his views and attitudes than any other Russian, more, almost, than any other European writer; nor can his art be called obscure in any normal sense: his universe has no dark corners, his stories are luminous with the light of day; he has explained them and himself, and argued about them and the methods by which they are constructed, more articulately and with greater force and sanity and lucidity than any other writer. Is he a fox or a hedgehog? What are we to say? Why is the answer so curiously difficult to find? Does he resemble Shakespeare or Pushkin more than Dante or Dostoevsky? Or is he wholly unlike either, and is the question therefore unanswerable because it is absurd? What is the mysterious obstacle with which our inquiry seems faced?

I do not propose in this essay to formulate a reply to this question, since this would involve nothing less than a critical examination of the art and thought of Tolstoy as a whole. I shall confine myself to suggesting that the difficulty may be, at least in part, due to the fact that Tolstoy was himself not unaware of the problem, and did his best to falsify the answer. The hypothesis I wish to offer is that Tolstoy was by nature a fox, but believed in being a hedgehog; that his gifts and achievement are one thing, and his beliefs, and consequently his interpretation of his own achievement, another; and that consequently his ideals have led him, and those whom his genius for persuasion has taken in, into a systematic misinterpretation of what he and others were doing or should be doing. No one can complain that he has left his readers in any doubt as to what he thought about this topic: his views on this subject permeate all his discursive writings—diaries, recorded *obiter dicta*, autobiographical essays and stories, social and religious tracts, literary criticism, letters to private and public correspondents. But the conflict between what he was and what he believed emerges nowhere so clearly as in his view of history to which some of his most brilliant and most paradoxical pages are devoted. This essay is an attempt to deal with his historical doctrines, and to consider both his motives for holding the views he holds and some of their probable sources. In short, it is an attempt to take Tolstoy's attitude to history as seriously as he himself meant his readers to take it, although for a somewhat different reason—for the light it casts on a single man of genius rather than on the fate of all mankind.

II

Tolstoy's philosophy of history has, on the whole, not obtained the attention which it deserves, whether as an intrinsically interesting view or as an occurrence in the history of ideas, or even as an element in the development of Tolstoy himself.[1] Those who have

[1] For the purpose of this essay I propose to confine myself almost entirely to the explicit philosophy of history contained in *War and Peace*, and to ignore, for example, *Sebastopol Stories*, *The Cossacks*, the fragments of the unpublished novel on the Decembrists, and Tolstoy's own scattered reflections on this subject except in so far as they bear on views expressed in *War and Peace*.

treated Tolstoy primarily as a novelist have at times looked upon the historical and philosophical passages scattered through *War and Peace* as so much perverse interruption of the narrative, as a regrettable liability to irrelevant digression characteristic of this great, but excessively opinionated, writer, a lop-sided, home-made metaphysic of small or no intrinsic interest, deeply inartistic and thoroughly foreign to the purpose and structure of the work of art as a whole. Turgenev, who found Tolstoy's personality and art antipathetic, although in later years he freely and generously acknowledged his genius as a writer, led the attack. In a letter to Pavel Annenkov[1] Turgenev speaks of Tolstoy's 'charlatanism', of his historical disquisitions as 'farcical', as 'trickery' which takes in the unwary, injected by an 'autodidact' into his work as an inadequate substitute for genuine knowledge. He hastens to add that Tolstoy does, of course, make up for this by 'his marvellous artistic genius'; and then accuses him of inventing 'a system which seems to solve everything very simply; as, for example, historical fatalism: he mounts his hobby-horse and is off! only when he touches earth does he, like Antaeus, recover his true strength.'[2] And the same note is sounded in the celebrated and touching invocation sent by Turgenev from his death-bed to his old friend and enemy, begging him to cast away his prophet's mantle and return to his true vocation—that of 'the great writer of the Russian land'. Flaubert, despite his 'shouts of joy and admiration' over passages of *War and Peace*, is equally horrified: 'il se répète! et il philosophise!' he writes in a letter to Turgenev who had sent him the French version of the masterpiece then almost unknown outside Russia. In the same strain

[1] See E. Bogoslavsky, *Turgenev o Tolstom* (Tiflis, 1894), p. 41; quoted by P. I. Biryukov, *L. N. Tolstoy* (Berlin, 1921), i. 48–9.

[2] Ibid.

Belinsky's intimate friend and correspondent, the philosophical tea-merchant, Vassili Botkin, who was well disposed to Tolstoy, writes to the poet Afanasi Fet: 'Literary specialists . . . find that the intellectual element of the novel is very weak, the philosophy of history is trivial and superficial, the denial of the decisive influence of individual personalities on events is nothing but a lot of mystical subtlety, but apart from this the artistic gift of the author is beyond dispute—yesterday I gave a dinner and Tyutchev was here, and I am repeating what everybody said.'[1] Contemporary historians and military specialists at least one of whom had himself fought in 1812,[2] indignantly complained of inaccuracies of fact; and since then damning evidence has been adduced of falsification of historical detail by the author of *War and Peace*,[3] done apparently with deliberate intent, in full knowledge of the available original sources and in the known absence of any counter-evidence—falsification perpetrated, it seems, in the interests not so much of an artistic as of an 'ideological' purpose. This consensus of historical and aesthetic criticism seems to have set the tone for nearly all later appraisals of the 'ideological' content of *War and Peace*. Shelgunov at least honoured it with a direct attack for its social quietism, which he called the 'philosophy of the

[1] A. Fet, *Moi vospominaniya* (St. Pbg., 1868), ii. 174.

[2] See the severe strictures of A. Vittmer, a very respectable military historian in his *1812 god v 'Voyne i Mire'* (St. Pbg., 1869), and the tones of mounting indignation in the contemporary critical notices of A. S. Norov, A. Pyatkovsky and C. Navalikhin. The first served in the campaign of 1812 and, despite some errors of fact, makes criticisms of substance. The last two are, as literary critics, almost worthless, but they seem to have taken the trouble to verify some of the relevant facts.

[3] See Viktor Shklovsky, *Material i stil' v romane L'va Tolstogo 'Voyna i Mir'* (Moscow, 1928), *passim*, but particularly ch. vii. See below, p. 28.

swamp'; others for the most part either politely ignored it, or treated it as a characteristic aberration which they put down to a combination of the well-known Russian tendency to preach (and thereby ruin works of art) with the half-baked infatuation with general ideas characteristic of young intellectuals in countries remote from centres of civilization. 'It is fortunate for us that the author is a better artist than thinker' said the critic Nikolai Akhsharumov,[1] and for more than three-quarters of a century this sentiment has been echoed by most of the critics of Tolstoy, both Russian and foreign, both pre-revolutionary and Soviet, both 'reactionary' and 'progressive', of those who look on him primarily as a writer and an artist, and of those to whom he is a prophet and a teacher, or a martyr, or a social influence, or a sociological or psychological 'case'. Tolstoy's theory of history is of equally little interest to Vogüé and Merezhkovsky, to Stefan Zweig and Mr. Percy Lubbock, to Biryukov and Professor Simmons, not to speak of lesser men. Historians of Russian thought[2] tend to label this aspect of Tolstoy as 'fatalism', and move on to the more interesting historical theories of Leontyev or Danilevsky. Critics endowed with more caution or humility do not go as far as this, but treat the 'philosophy' with nervous respect; even Mr. Derrick Leon, who treats Tolstoy's views of this period with greater care than the majority of his biographers, after giving a painstaking account of Tolstoy's reflections on the forces which dominate history, particularly of the second section of the long epilogue which follows the end of the narrative portion of *War and Peace*, proceeds to follow the late Aylmer Maude in making no attempt either to assess the theory or to relate it to the rest of Tolstoy's life or

[1] *Razbor 'Voyny i Mira'* (St. Pbg., 1868), pp. 1–4.
[2] e.g. Professors Ilyin, Yakovenko, Zen'kovsky and others.

[7]

thought; and even so much as this is almost unique.[1] Those, again, who are mainly interested in Tolstoy as a prophet and a teacher concentrate on the later doctrines of the master, held after his conversion, when he had ceased to regard himself primarily as a writer and had established himself as a teacher of mankind, an object of veneration and pilgrimage. Tolstoy's life is normally represented as falling into two distinct parts; first comes the author of immortal masterpieces, later the prophet of personal and social regeneration; first the aristocratic writer, the difficult, somewhat unapproachable, troubled novelist of genius; then the sage, dogmatic perverse, exaggerated, but wielding a vast influence, particularly in his own country—a world institution of unique importance. From time to time attempts are made to trace his later period to its roots in his earlier phase which is felt to be full of pre-sentiments of the later life of self-renunciation; it is this later period which is regarded as important; there are philosophical, theological, ethical, psychological, political, economic studies of the later Tolstoy in all his aspects.

And yet there is surely a paradox here. Tolstoy's

[1] Honourable exceptions to this are provided by the writings of the Russian writers N. Kareyev and B. Eykhenbaum, as well as those of the French scholars E. Haumant and Albert Sorel. Of monographs devoted to this subject I know of only two of any worth. The first—'Filosofiya istorii L. N. Tolstogo', by V. Pertsev, in 'Voyna i Mir': sbornik pamyati L. Tolstogo, ed. T. I. Polner and V. P. Obninsky (Moscow, Zadruga, 1912), after taking Tolstoy mildly to task for obscurities, exaggerations and inconsistencies, swiftly retreats into innocuous generalities. The other—'Filosofiya istorii v romane L. N. Tolstogo', Voyna i Mir, by M. M. Rubin-shteyn in Russkaya Mysl', July 1911, is much more laboured, but in end, seems to me to establish nothing at all. As for the inevitable efforts to relate Tolstoy's historical views to those of various latter-day Marxists—Kautsky, Lenin, Stalin, etc.—they belong to the curiosities of politics or theology rather than to those of literature.

interest in history and the problem of historical truth was passionate, almost obsessive, both before and during the writing of *War and Peace*. No one who reads his journals and letters, or indeed *War and Peace* itself, can doubt that the author himself, at any rate, regarded this problem as the heart of the entire matter—the central issue round which the novel is built. 'Charlatanism', 'superficiality', 'intellectual feebleness'—surely Tolstoy is the last writer to whom these epithets seem applicable: bias, perversity, arrogance, perhaps; self-deception, lack of restraint, possibly; moral or spiritual inadequacy—of this he was better aware than his enemies; but failure of intellect —lack of critical power—a tendency to emptiness— liability to ride off on some patently absurd, superficial doctrine to the detriment of realistic description or analysis of life—infatuation with some fashionable theory which Botkin or Fet can easily see through, although Tolstoy, alas, cannot—these charges seem grotesquely unplausible. No man in his senses, during this century at any rate, would ever dream of denying Tolstoy's intellectual power, his appalling capacity to penetrate any conventional disguise, that corrosive scepticism in virtue of which Prince Vyazemsky invented for him the queer Russian term 'netovshchik'[1] ('negativist')—an early version of that nihilism which Vogüé and Albert Sorel later quite naturally attribute to him. Something is surely amiss here: Tolstoy's violently unhistorical and indeed anti-historical rejection of all efforts to explain or justify human action or character in terms of social or individual growth, or 'roots' in the past; this side by side with an absorbed and life-long interest in history, leading to artistic and philosophical results which provoked such queerly disparaging comments from ordinarily sane and

[1] See article by M. de Poulet in *Sankt-Petersburgskiya Vedomosti*, 1869, No. 144.

[9]

sympathetic critics—surely there is something here which deserves attention.

III

Tolstoy's interest in history began early in his life. It seems to have arisen not from interest in the past as such, but from the desire to penetrate to first causes, to understand how and why things happen as they do and not otherwise, from discontent with those current explanations which do not explain, and leave the mind dissatisfied, from a tendency to doubt and place under suspicion and, if need be, reject whatever does not fully answer the question, to go to the root of every matter, at whatever cost. This remained Tolstoy's attitude throughout his entire life, and is scarcely a symptom either of 'trickery' or of 'superficiality'. And with this went an incurable love of the concrete, the empirical, the verifiable, and an instinctive distrust of the abstract, the impalpable, the supernatural—in short an early tendency to a scientific and positivist approach, unfriendly to romanticism, abstract formulations, metaphysics. Always and in every situation he looked for 'hard' facts—for what could be grasped and verified by the normal intellect uncorrupted by intricate theories divorced from tangible realities, or by other-wordly mysteries, theological, poetical, and metaphysical alike. He was tormented by the ultimate problems which face young men in every generation—about good and evil, the origin and purpose of the universe and its inhabitants, the causes of all that happens; but the answers provided by theologians and metaphysicians struck him as absurd, if only because of the words in which they were formulated—words which bore no apparent reference to the everyday world of ordinary common sense to which he clung obstinately, even before he became aware of what he was doing, as being alone real. History, only history, only the sum of the concrete events in time and space—the sum of the actual experience of actual men and women in their relation to one another and to an actual, three-dimensional, empirically experienced, physical environment—this alone contained the truth, the material out of which genuine answers—answers needing for their apprehension no special senses or faculties which normal human beings did not possess—might be constructed. This, of course, was the spirit of empirical inquiry which animated the great anti-theological and anti-metaphysical thinkers of the eighteenth century, and Tolstoy's realism and inability to be taken in by shadows made him their natural disciple before he had learnt of their doctrines. Like M. Jourdain, he spoke prose long before he knew it, and remained an enemy of transcendentalism from the beginning to the end of his life. He grew up during the hey-day of the Hegelian philosophy which sought to explain all things in terms of historical development, but conceived this process as being ultimately not susceptible to the methods of empirical investigation. The historicism of his time doubtless influenced the young Tolstoy as it did all inquiring persons of his time; but the metaphysical content he rejected instinctively, and in one of his letters he described Hegel's writings as unintelligible gibberish interspersed with platitudes. History alone—the sum of empirically discoverable data—held the key to the mystery of why what happened happened as it did and not otherwise; and only history, consequently, could throw light on the fundamental ethical problems which obsessed him as it did every Russian thinker in the nineteenth century. What is to be done? How should one live? Why are we here? What must we be and do? the study of historical connexions and the demand for empirical answers to these 'proklyatye voprosy'[1] became fused into one in Tolstoy's mind, as his early diaries and letters show very vividly.

In his early diaries (1846–53)[2] we find references to his attempts to compare Catherine the Great's *Nakaz*[3] with the passages in Montesquieu on which she professed to have founded it. He reads Hume and Thiers[4] as well as Rousseau, Sterne, and Dickens. He is obsessed by the thought that philosophical principles can only be understood in their concrete expression in history.[5] 'To write the genuine history of present-day Europe: there is an aim for the whole of one's life.'[6] Or again: 'The leaves of a tree delight us more than the roots',[7] with the implication that this is nevertheless a superficial view of the world. But side by side with this there is the beginning of an acute sense of disappointment, a feeling that history, as it is written by historians, makes claims which it cannot satisfy, because like metaphysical philosophy it pretends to be something it is not—namely, a science capable of arriving at conclusions which are certain. Since men cannot solve philosophical questions by the principles of reason they try to do so historically. But history is 'one of the most backward of sciences—a science

[1] 'Accursed questions'—a phrase which became a cliché in nineteenth-century Russia for those central moral and social issues of which every honest man, in particular every writer, must sooner or later become aware, and then be faced with the choice of either entering the struggle or of turning his back upon his fellow-men, conscious of his responsibility for what he was doing.

[2] L. N. Tolstoy, *Polnoe sobranie sochineniy*, ed. V. G. Chertkov (Jubilee edn., Moscow, 1934), xlvi, pp. 4–28 (1847) and pp. 97, 113, 114, 117, 123–4, 127, 132 (1852).

[3] Instructions to her legislative experts.

[4] N. Apostolov, *Lev Tolstoy nad stranitsami istorii* (Moscow, 1928), p. 18.

[5] L. Tolstoy, *Dnevnik molodosti*, ed. V. G. Chertkov, p. 132.

[6] Ibid., p. 154.

[7] Apostolov, op. cit., p. 20.

which has lost its proper aim'.[1] The reason for this is that history will not, because it cannot, solve the great questions which have tormented men in every generation. In the course of seeking to answer these questions men accumulate a knowledge of facts as they succeed each other in time: but this is a mere by-product, a kind of 'side issue' which—and this is a mistake—is studied as an end in itself. And again, 'history will never reveal to us what connexions there are, and at what times, between science, art, and morality, between good and evil, religion and the civic virtues . . . What it *will* tell us (and that incorrectly) is where the Huns came from, when they lived, who laid the foundations of their power, etc.' And Tolstoy observes in the summer of 1852 to his friend Nazar'ev: 'History is nothing but a collection of fables and useless trifles, cluttered up with a mass of unnecessary figures and proper names. The death of Igor, the snake which bit Oleg—what is all this but old wives' tales? Who wants to know that Ivan's second marriage, to Temryuk's daughter, occurred on August 21, 1562, whereas his fourth, to Anna Alekseyevna Koltovskaya, occurred in 1572. . . .'[2]

History does not reveal causes; it presents only a blank succession of unexplained events. 'Everything is forced into a standard mould invented by the historians: Tsar Ivan the Terrible, on whom Professor Ivanov is lecturing at the moment, after 1560 suddenly becomes transformed from a wise and virtuous man into a mad and cruel tyrant. How? Why?—You mustn't even ask. . . .' And half a century later, in 1908, he declares to Gusev: 'History would be an excellent thing if only it were true.'[3] The proposition that

[1] Apostolov, op. cit., p. 20.

[2] V. N. Nazar'ev, 'Zhizn' i lyudi bylogo vremeni', in *Istoricheski Vestnik*, Nov. 1900.

[3] N. N. Gusev, *Dva goda s Tolstym* (Moscow, 1912), p. 175.

history could (and should) be made scientific is a commonplace in the nineteenth century; but the number of those who interpreted the term 'science' as meaning natural science, and then asked themselves whether history could be transformed into a science in this specific sense, is not great. The most uncompromising policy was that of Auguste Comte, who, following his master, Saint-Simon, tried to turn history into sociology, with what fantastic consequences we need not here relate. Karl Marx was perhaps, of all thinkers, the man who took this programme most seriously; and made the bravest, if one of the least successful, attempts to discover general laws which govern historical evolution, conceived on the then alluring analogy of biology and anatomy so triumphantly transformed by Darwin's new evolutionary theories. Like Marx (of whom at the time of writing *War and Peace* he apparently knew nothing) Tolstoy saw clearly that if history was a science, it must be possible to discover and formulate a set of true laws of history which, in conjunction with the data of empirical observation, would make prediction of the future (and 'retrodiction' of the past) as feasible as it had become, say, in geology or astronomy. But he saw more clearly than Marx and his followers that this had, in fact, not been achieved, and said so with his usual dogmatic candour, and reinforced his thesis with arguments designed to show that the prospect of achieving this goal was non-existent; and clinched the matter by observing that the fulfilment of this scientific hope would end human life as we knew it: 'if we allow that human life can be ruled by reason, the possibility of life [i.e. as a spontaneous activity involving consciousness of free will][1] is destroyed'.[2] But what oppressed Tolstoy was not merely the 'unscientific' nature of

[1] My brackets.

[2] *War and Peace*, Epilogue, pt. i, section i.

[14]

history—that no matter how scrupulous the technique of historical research might be, no dependable laws could be discovered of the kind required even by the most undeveloped natural sciences—but he further thought that he could not justify to himself the apparently arbitrary selection of material, and the no less arbitrary distribution of emphasis, to which all historical writing seemed to be doomed. He complains that while the factors which determine the life of mankind are very various, historians select from them only some single aspect, say the political or the economic, and represent it as primary, as the efficient cause of social change; but then, what of religion, what of 'spiritual' factors, and the many other aspects—a literally countless multiplicity—with which all events are endowed? How can we escape the conclusion that the histories which exist represent what Tolstoy declares to be 'perhaps only ·001 per cent of the elements which actually constitute the real history of peoples'. History, as it is normally written, usually represents 'political'—public—events as the most important, while spiritual—'inner'—events are largely forgotten; yet *prima facie* it is they—the 'inner' events—that are the most real, the most immediate experience of human beings; they, and only they, are what life, in the last analysis, is made of; hence the routine political historians are talking shallow nonsense.

Throughout the fifties Tolstoy was obsessed by the desire to write a historical novel, one of his principal aims being to contrast the 'real' texture of life, both of individuals and communities, with the 'unreal' picture presented by historians. Again and again in the pages of *War and Peace* we get a sharp juxtaposition of 'reality'—what 'really' occurred—with the distorting medium through which it will later be presented in the official accounts offered to the public, and indeed

[15]

be recollected by the actors themselves—the original memories having now been touched up by their own treacherous (inevitably treacherous because automatically rationalizing and formalizing) minds. Tolstoy is perpetually placing the heroes of *War and Peace* in situations where this becomes particularly evident.

Nikolai Rostov at the battle of Austerlitz sees the great soldier, Prince Bagration, riding up with his suite towards the village of Schöngraben whence the enemy is advancing; neither he nor his staff, nor the officers who gallop up to him with messages, nor anyone else is, or can be, aware of what exactly is happening, nor where, nor why; nor is the chaos of the battle in any way made clearer either in fact or in the minds of the Russian officers by the appearance of Bagration. Nevertheless his arrival puts heart into his subordinates; his courage, his calm, his mere presence create the illusion of which he is himself the first victim, namely, that what is happening is somehow connected with *his* skill, *his* plans, that it is *his* authority that is in some way directing the course of the battle; and this, in its turn, has a marked effect on the general morale all round him. The dispatches which will duly be written later will inevitably ascribe every act and event on the Russian side to him and his dispositions; the credit or discredit, the victory or the defeat will belong to him, although it is clear to everyone that he will have had less to do with the conduct and outcome of the battle than the humble, unknown soldiers who do at least perform whatever actual fighting is done, i.e. shoot at each other, wound, kill, advance, retreat, and so on.

Prince Andrey, too, knows this, most clearly at Borodino where he is mortally wounded. He begins to understand the truth earlier, during the period when he is making efforts to meet the 'important' persons who seem to be guiding the destinies of Russia; he then gradually becomes convinced that Alexander's principal adviser, the famous reformer Speransky, and his friends, and indeed Alexander himself, are systematically deluding themselves when they suppose their activities, their words, memoranda, rescripts, resolutions, laws, etc., to be the motive factors which cause historical change and determine the destinies of men and nations; whereas in fact they are nothing; only so much self-important milling in the void. And so Tolstoy arrives at one of his celebrated paradoxes: the higher soldiers or statesmen are in the pyramid of authority, the farther they must be from its base which consists of those ordinary men and women whose lives are the actual stuff of history; and, consequently, the smaller the effect of the words and acts of such remote personages, despite all their theoretical authority, upon that history. In a famous passage dealing with the state of Moscow in 1812 Tolstoy observes that from the heroic achievements of Russia after the burning of Moscow one might infer that its inhabitants were absorbed entirely in acts of self-sacrifice—in saving their country, or in lamenting its destruction—in heroism, martyrdom, despair, etc., but that in fact this was not so. People were preoccupied by personal interests. Those who went about their ordinary business without feeling heroic emotions or thinking that they were actors upon the well-lighted stage of history, were the most useful to their country and community, while those who tried to grasp the general course of events and wanted to take part in history, those who performed acts of incredible self-sacrifice or heroism, and participated in great events, were the most useless.[1] Worst of all, in Tolstoy's eyes, were those unceasing talkers who accused one another of the kind of thing 'for which no one could in fact have been

[1] *War and Peace*, vol. IV, pt. i, ch. iv.

responsible'. And this because 'nowhere is the commandment not to taste of the fruit of the tree of knowledge so clearly written as in the course of history. Only unconscious activity bears fruit, and the individual who plays a part in historical events never understands their significance. If he attempts to understand them, he is struck with sterility.'[1] To try to 'understand' anything by rational means is to make sure of failure. Pierre Bezukhov wanders about, 'lost' on the battlefield of Borodino, and looks for something which he imagines as a kind of set piece; a battle as depicted by the historians or the painters. But he finds only the ordinary confusion of individual human beings haphazardly attending to this or that human want.[2] That, at any rate, is concrete, uncontaminated by theories and abstractions; and Pierre is therefore closer to the truth about the course of events—at least as seen by men—than those who believe them to obey a discoverable set of laws or rules. Pierre sees only a succession of 'accidents' whose origins and consequences are, by and large, untraceable and unpredictable; only loosely strung groups of events forming an ever varying pattern, following no discernible order. Any claim to perceive patterns susceptible to 'scientific' formulae must be mendacious.

Tolstoy's bitterest taunts, his most corrosive irony are reserved for those who pose as official specialists in managing human affairs, in this case the Western military theorists, a General Pfuel, or Generals Bennigsen and Paulucci, who are all shown talking equal nonsense at the Council of Drissa, whether they defend a given strategic or tactical theory or oppose it; these men must be impostors since no theories can possibly fit the immense variety of possible human behaviour,

[1] Ibid.

[2] On the connection of this with Stendhal's *La Chartreuse de Parme* see footnote [1] on p. 47.

the vast multiplicity of minute, undiscoverable causes and effects which form that interplay of men and nature which history purports to record. Those who affect to be able to contract this infinite multiplicity within their 'scientific' laws must be either deliberate charlatans, or blind leaders of the blind. The harshest judgement is accordingly reserved for the master theorist himself, the great Napoleon, who acts upon, and has hypnotized others into believing, the assumption that he understands and controls events by his superior intellect, or by flashes of intuition, or by otherwise succeeding in answering correctly the problems posed by history. The greater the claim the greater the lie: Napoleon is consequently the most pitiable, the most contemptible of all the actors in the great tragedy.

This, then, is the great illusion which Tolstoy sets himself to expose: that individuals can, by the use of their own resources, understand and control the course of events. Those who believe this turn out to be dreadfully mistaken. And side by side with these public faces—these hollow men, half self-deluded, half aware of being fraudulent, talking, writing, desperately and aimlessly in order to keep up appearances and avoid facing the bleak truths—side by side with all this elaborate machinery for concealing the spectacle of human impotence and irrelevance and blindness lies the real world, the stream of life which men understand, the attending to the ordinary details of daily existence. When Tolstoy contrasts this real life—the actual, everyday, 'live' experience of individuals—with the panoramic view conjured up by historians, it is clear to him which is real, and which is a coherent, sometimes elegantly contrived, but always fictitious construction. Utterly unlike her as he is in almost every other respect, Tolstoy is, perhaps, the first to propound the celebrated accusation which Virginia Woolf half a century later levelled against the public prophets of her own generation—Shaw and Wells and Arnold Bennett—blind materialists who did not begin to understand what it is that life truly consists of, who mistook its outer accidents, the unimportant aspects which lie outside the individual soul—the so-called social, economic, political realities—for that which alone is genuine, the individual experience, the specific relation of individuals to one another, the colours, smells, tastes, sounds, and movements, the jealousies, loves, hatreds, passions, the rare flashes of insight, the transforming moments, the ordinary day-to-day succession of private data which constitute all there is— which are reality.

What, then, is the historian's task—to describe the ultimate data of subjective experience—the personal lives lived by men—the 'thoughts, knowledge, poetry, music, love, friendship, hates, passions' of which, for Tolstoy, 'real' life is compounded, and only that? That was the task to which Turgenev was perpetually calling Tolstoy—him and all writers, but him in particular, because therein lay his true genius, his destiny as a great Russian writer; and this he rejected with violent indignation even during his middle years, before the final religious phase. For this was not to give the answer to the question of what there is, and why and how it comes to be and passes away, but to turn one's back upon it altogether, and stifle one's desire to discover how men live in society, and how they are affected by one another and by their environment, and to what end. This kind of artistic purism— preached in his day by Flaubert—this kind of preoccupation with the analysis and description of the experience and the relationships and problems and inner lives of individuals (later advocated and practised by Gide and the writers he influenced, both in France and in England) struck him as both trivial and false. He had no doubt about his own superlative skill in this very art—and that it was precisely this for which he was admired; and he condemned it absolutely. In a letter written while he was working on *War and Peace* he said with bitterness that he had no doubt that what the public would like best would be his scenes of social and personal life, his ladies and his gentlemen, with their petty intrigues, and entertaining conversations and marvellously described small idiosyncrasies.[1] But these are the trivial 'flowers' of life, not the 'roots'. Tolstoy's purpose is the discovery of the truth, and therefore he must know what history consists of, and recreate only that. History is plainly not a science, and sociology, which pretends that it is, is a fraud; no genuine laws of history have been discovered, and the concepts in current use—'cause', 'accident', 'genius'—explain nothing: they are merely thin disguises for ignorance. Why do the events the totality of which we call history occur as they do? Some historians attribute events to the acts of individuals, but this is no answer: for they do not explain how these acts 'cause' the events they are alleged to 'cause' or 'originate'. There is a passage of savage irony intended by Tolstoy to parody the average school histories of his time, sufficiently typical to be worth reproducing in full:[2]

'Louis XIV was a very proud and self-confident man. He had such and such mistresses, and such and such ministers, and they governed France badly. The heirs of Louis XIV were also weak men, and also governed France badly. They also had such and such favourites and such and such mistresses. Besides which, certain persons were at this time

[1] Cf. the profession of faith in his celebrated—and militantly moralistic—introduction to an edition of Maupassant whose genius, despite everything, he admires. He thinks much more poorly of Bernard Shaw whose social rhetoric he calls stale and platitudinous.

[2] *War and Peace*, Epilogue, pt. ii, ch. i.

writing books. By the end of the eighteenth century there must have gathered in Paris two dozen or so persons who started saying that all men were free and equal. Because of this in the whole of France people began to slaughter and drown each other. These people killed the king and a good many others. At this time there was a man of genius in France—Napoleon. He conquered everyone everywhere, i.e. killed a great many people because he was a great genius; and, for some reason, he went off to kill Africans, and killed them so well, and was so clever and cunning, that, having arrived in France, he ordered everyone to obey him, which they did. Having made himself Emperor he again went to kill masses of people in Italy, Austria and Prussia. And there too he killed a great many. Now in Russia there was the Emperor Alexander who decided to re-establish order in Europe, and therefore fought wars with Napoleon. But in the year '07 he suddenly made friends with him, and in the year '11 quarrelled with him again, and they both again began to kill a great many people. And Napoleon brought six hundred thousand men to Russia and conquered Moscow. But then he suddenly ran away from Moscow, and then the Emperor Alexander, aided by the advice of Stein and others, united Europe to raise an army against the disturber of her peace. Napoleon's allies suddenly became his enemies; and this army marched against Napoleon, who had gathered new forces. The allies conquered Napoleon, entered Paris, forced Napoleon to renounce the throne, and sent him to the island of Elba, without, however, depriving him of the title of Emperor, and showing him all respect, in spite of the fact that five years before and a year after, everyone considered him a brigand and beyond the law. Thereupon Louis XVIII, who until then had been an object of mere ridicule to both Frenchmen and the allies, began to reign. As for Napoleon, after shedding tears before the Old Guard, he gave up his throne, and went into exile. Then astute statesmen and diplomats, in particular Talleyrand, who had managed to sit down before anyone else in the famous arm-chair[1] and thereby to extend the frontiers of France, talked

[1] Empire chairs of a certain shape are to this day called 'Talleyrand armchairs' in Russia.

in Vienna, and by means of such talk made peoples happy or unhappy. Suddenly the diplomats and monarchs almost came to blows. They were almost ready to order their troops once again to kill each other; but at this moment Napoleon arrived in France with a battalion, and the French, who hated him, all immediately submitted to him. But this annoyed the allied monarchs very much and they again went to war with the French. And the genius Napoleon was defeated and taken to the island of St. Helena, having suddenly been discovered to be an outlaw. Whereupon the exile, parted from his dear ones and his beloved France, died a slow death on a rock, and bequeathed his great deeds to posterity. As for Europe, a reaction occurred there, and all the princes began to treat their peoples badly once again.'

Tolstoy continues:

'The new history is like a deaf man replying to questions which nobody puts to him . . . The primary question is, what power is it that moves the destinies of peoples? . . . History seems to presuppose that this power can be taken for granted, and is familiar to everyone, but, in spite of every wish to admit that this power is familiar to us, anyone who has read a great many historical works cannot help doubting whether this power, which different historians understand in different ways, is in fact so completely familiar to everyone.'

He goes on to say that political historians who write in this way explain nothing; they merely attribute events to the 'power' which important individuals are said to exercise on others, but do not tell us what the term 'power' means: and yet this is the heart of the problem. The problem of historical movement is directly connected with the 'power' exercised by some men over others: but what is 'power'? How does one acquire it? Can it be transferred by one man to another? Surely it is not merely physical strength that is meant? Nor moral strength? Did Napoleon possess either of these? General, as opposed to national, historians seem to Tolstoy merely to extend this category without elucidating it: instead of one country or nation, many are introduced, but the spectacle of the interplay of mysterious 'forces' makes it no clearer why some men or nations obey others, why wars are made, victories won, why innocent men who believe that murder is wicked kill one another with enthusiasm and pride, and are glorified for so doing; why great movements of human masses occur, sometimes from east to west, sometimes the other way. Tolstoy is particularly irritated by references to the dominant influence of great men or of ideas. Great men, we are told, are typical of the movements of their age: hence study of their characters 'explains' such movements. Do the characters of Diderot or Beaumarchais 'explain' the advance of the West upon the East? do the letters of Ivan the Terrible to Prince Kurbsky 'explain' Russian expansion westward? But historians of culture do no better, for they merely add as an extra factor something called the 'force' of ideas or of books, although we still have no notion of what is meant by words like 'force'. But why should Napoleon, or Mme de Staël or Baron Stein or Tsar Alexander, or all of these, plus the *Contrat Social*, 'cause' Frenchmen to behead or to drown each other? Why is this called an 'explanation'? As for the importance which historians of culture attach to ideas, doubtless all men are liable to exaggerate the importance of their own wares: ideas are the commodity in which intellectuals deal—to a cobbler there's nothing like leather—the professors merely tend to magnify their personal activities into the central 'force' that rules the world. Tolstoy adds that an even deeper darkness is cast upon this subject by political theorists, moralists, metaphysicians. The celebrated notion of the social contract, for example, which some liberals peddle, speaks of the 'vesting' of the wills, i.e. the power, of many men in one individual or group of individuals; but what kind of act is this 'vesting'? It may have a legal or ethical significance, it may be relevant to what should be considered as permitted or forbidden, to the world of rights and duties, or of the good and the bad, but as a factual explanation of how a sovereign accumulates enough 'power'—as if it were a commodity—which enables him to effect this or that result, it means nothing. It declares that the conferring of power makes powerful; but this tautology is too unilluminating. What is 'power' and what is 'conferring'? and who confers it and how is such conferring done?[1] The process seems very different from whatever it is that is discussed by the physical sciences. Conferring is an act, but an unintelligible one; conferring power, acquiring it, using it, is not at all like eating or drinking or thinking or walking. We remain in the dark: *obscurum per obscurius*.

After demolishing the jurists and moralists and political philosophers—among them his beloved Rousseau—Tolstoy applies himself to demolishing the liberal theory of history according to which everything may turn upon what may seem an insignificant accident. Hence the pages in which he obstinately tries to prove that Napoleon knew as little of what actually went on during the battle of Borodino as the lowliest of his soldiers; and that therefore his cold on the eve of it, of which so much was made by the historians, could have made no appreciable difference. With great force he argues that only those orders or decisions issued by the commanders now seem particularly crucial (and are concentrated upon by historians), which happened to coincide with what

[1] One of Tolstoy's Russian critics, M. Rubinshteyn, referred to on p. 8, footnote 1, says that every science employs *some* unanalysed concepts, to explain which is the business of other sciences; and that 'power' happens to be the unexplained central concept of history. But Tolstoy's point is that no other science can 'explain' it, since it is, as used by historians, a meaningless term, not a concept but nothing at all—*vox nihili*.

later actually occurred; whereas a great many other exactly similar, perfectly good orders and decisions, which seemed no less crucial and vital to those who were issuing them at the time, are forgotten because, having been foiled by unfavourable turns of events, they were not, because they could not be, carried out, and for this reason now seem historically unimportant. After disposing of the heroic theory of history, Tolstoy turns with even greater savagery upon scientific sociology, which claims to have discovered laws of history, but cannot possibly have found any, because the number of causes upon which events turn is too great for human knowledge or calculation. We know too few facts, and we select them at random and in accordance with our subjective inclinations. No doubt if we were omniscient we might be able, like Laplace's ideal observer, to plot the course of every drop of which the stream of history consists, but we are, of course, pathetically ignorant, and the areas of our knowledge are incredibly small compared to what is uncharted and (Tolstoy vehemently insists on this) unchartable. Freedom of the will is an illusion which cannot be shaken off, but, as great philosophers have said, it is an illusion nevertheless, and it derives solely from ignorance of true causes. The more we know about the circumstances of an act, the farther away from us the act is in time, the more difficult it is to think away its consequences; the more solidly embedded a fact is in the actual world in which we live, the less we can imagine how things might have turned out if something different had happened. For by now it seems inevitable: to think otherwise would upset too much of our world order. The more closely we relate an act to its context, the less free the actor seems to be, the less responsible for his act, and the less disposed we are to hold him accountable or blameworthy. The fact that we shall never identify all the causes, relate all human acts to the circumstances which condition them, does not imply that they are free, only that we shall never know how they are necessitated.

Tolstoy's central thesis—in some respects not unlike the theory of the inevitable 'self-deception' of the *bourgeoisie* held by his contemporary Karl Marx, save that what Marx reserves for a class, Tolstoy sees in almost all mankind—is that there is a natural law whereby the lives of human beings no less than those of nature are determined; but that men, unable to face this inexorable process, seek to represent it as a succession of free choices, to fix responsibility for what occurs upon persons endowed by them with heroic virtues or heroic vices, and called by them 'great men'. What are great men? they are ordinary human beings, who are ignorant and vain enough to accept responsibility for the life of society, individuals who would rather take the blame for all the cruelties, injustices, disasters justified in their name, than recognize their own insignificance and impotence in the cosmic flow which pursues its course irrespective of their wills and ideals. This is the central point of those passages (in which Tolstoy excelled) in which the actual course of events is described, side by side with the absurd, egocentric explanations which persons blown up with the sense of their own importance necessarily give to them; as well as of the wonderful descriptions of moments of illumination in which the truth about the human condition dawns upon those who have the humility to recognize their own unimportance and irrelevance. And this is the purpose, too, of those philosophical passages where, in language more ferocious than Spinoza's, but with intentions similar to his, the errors of the pseudo-sciences are exposed. There is a particularly vivid simile[1] in which the great man is likened to the

---

[1] *War and Peace*, Epilogue, pt. i, ch. ii.

ram whom the shepherd is fattening for slaughter. Because the ram duly grows fatter, and perhaps is used as a bell-wether for the rest of the flock, he may easily imagine that he is the leader of the flock, and that the other sheep go where they go solely in obedience to his will. He thinks this and the flock may think it too. Nevertheless the purpose of his selection is not the rôle he believes himself to play, but slaughter—a purpose conceived by beings whose aims neither he nor the other sheep can fathom. For Tolstoy Napoleon is just such a ram, and so to some degree is Alexander, and indeed all the great men of history. Indeed, as an acute literary historian has pointed out,[1] Tolstoy sometimes seems almost deliberately to ignore the historical evidence and more than once consciously distorts the facts in order to bolster up his favourite thesis. The character of Kutuzov is a case in point. Such heroes as Pierre Bezukhov or Karataev are at least imaginary, and Tolstoy had an undisputed right to endow them with all the attributes he admired—humility, freedom from bureaucratic or scientific or other rationalistic kinds of blindness. But Kutuzov was a real person, and it is all the more instructive to observe the steps by which he transforms him from the sly, elderly, feeble voluptuary, the corrupt and somewhat sycophantic courtier of the early drafts of *War and Peace* which were based on authentic sources, into the unforgettable symbol of the Russian people in all its simplicity and intuitive wisdom. By the time we reach the celebrated passage—one of the most moving in literature—in which Tolstoy describes the moment when the old man is woken in his camp at Fili to be told that the French army is retreating, we have left the facts behind us, and are in an imaginary realm, a historical and

[1] See V. Shklovsky, op. cit., p. 6, note 3, chs. vii–ix, and also K. Pokrovsky, 'Istochniki romana *Voyna i Mir*' in *Voyna i Mir*, ed. Polner and Obninsky, op. cit., p. 8, note 1.

emotional atmosphere for which the evidence is flimsy, but which is artistically indispensable to Tolstoy's design. The final apotheosis of Kutuzov is totally unhistorical for all Tolstoy's repeated professions of his undeviating devotion to the sacred cause of the truth. In *War and Peace* Tolstoy treats facts cavalierly when it suits him, because he is above all obsessed by his thesis —the contrast between the universal and all-important but delusive experience of free will, the feeling of responsibility, the values of private life generally, on the one hand; and on the other, the reality of inexorable historical determinism, not, indeed, experienced directly, but known to be true on irrefutable theoretical grounds. This corresponds in its turn to a tormenting inner conflict, one of many, in Tolstoy himself, between the two systems of value, the public and the private. On the one hand, if those feelings and immediate experiences, upon which the ordinary values of private individuals and historians alike ultimately rest, are nothing but a vast illusion, this must, in the name of the truth, be ruthlessly demonstrated, and the values and the explanations which derive from the illusion exposed and discredited. And in a sense Tolstoy does try to do this, particularly when he is philosophizing, as in the great public scenes of the novel itself, the battle pieces, the descriptions of the movements of peoples, the metaphysical disquisitions. But, on the other hand, he also does the exact opposite of this when he contrasts with this panorama of public life the superior value of personal experience, the 'thoughts, knowledge, poetry, music, love, friendship, hates, passions' of which real life is compounded— when he contrasts the concrete and multi-coloured reality of individual lives with the pale abstractions of scientists or historians, particularly the latter, 'from Gibbon to Buckle', whom he denounces so harshly for mistaking their own empty categories for real facts.

And yet the primacy of these private experiences and relationships and virtues presupposes that vision of life, with its sense of personal responsibility, and belief in freedom and possibility of spontaneous action, to which the best pages of *War and Peace* are devoted, and which is the very illusion to be exorcized, if the truth is to be faced.

This terrible dilemma is never finally resolved. Sometimes, as in the explanation of his intentions which he published before the final part of *War and Peace* had appeared,[1] Tolstoy vacillates; the individual is 'in some sense' free when he alone is involved: thus, in raising his arm, he is free within physical limits. But once he is involved in relationships with others, he is no longer free, he is part of the inexorable stream. Freedom is real, but it is confined to trivial acts. At other times even this feeble ray of hope is extinguished: Tolstoy declares that he cannot admit even small exceptions to the universal law; causal determinism is either wholly pervasive or it is nothing, and chaos reigns. Men's acts may seem free of the social nexus, but they are not free, they cannot be free, they are part of it. Science cannot destroy the consciousness of freedom, without which there is no morality and no art, but it can refute it. 'Power' and 'accident' are but names for ignorance of the causal chains, but the chains exist whether we feel them or not; fortunately we do not; for if we felt their weight, we could scarcely act at all; the loss of the illusion would paralyse the life which is lived on the basis of our happy ignorance. But all is well: for we never shall discover all the causal chains that operate: the number of such causes is infinitely great, the causes themselves infinitely small; historians select an absurdly small portion of them and attribute everything to this arbitrarily chosen tiny

[1] 'Neskol'ko slov po povodu knigi *Voyna i Mir*', in *Russki Arkhiv*, 1868, coll. 515–28.

section. How would an ideal historical science operate? By using a kind of calculus whereby this 'differential', the infinitesimals—the infinitely small human and non-human actions and events—would be integrated, and in this way the continuum of history would no longer be distorted by being broken up into arbitrary segments.[1] Tolstoy expresses this notion of calculation by infinitesimals with great lucidity, and with his habitual simple, vivid, precise use of words. The late M. Henri Bergson, who made his name with his theory of the flow of events which the artificial fragmentation, such as is made in the natural sciences, distorts, 'kills', and so on, developed a very similar point at infinitely greater length, less clearly, less plausibly, and with an unnecessary parade of terminology.

It is not a mystical or an intuitionist view of life. Our ignorance of how things happen is not due to some inherent inaccessibility of the first causes, only to their multiplicity, the smallness of the ultimate units, and our own inability to see and hear and remember and record and co-ordinate enough of the available material. Omniscience is in principle possible even to empirical beings, but, of course, in practice unattainable. This alone, and nothing deeper or more interesting, is the source of human megalomania, of all our absurd delusions. Since we are not, in fact, free, but could not live without the conviction that we are, what are we to do? Tolstoy arrives at no clear conclusion, only at the view, in some respect like Burke's, that it is better to realize that we understand what goes on as we do in fact understand it—much as spontaneous, normal, simple people, uncorrupted by theories, not blinded by the dust raised by the scientific authorities, do, in fact, understand life—than to

[1] *War and Peace*, vol. III, pt. iii, ch. i.

seek to subvert such common-sense beliefs, which at least have the merit of having been tested by long experience, in favour of pseudo-sciences, which, being founded on absurdly inadequate data, are only a snare and a delusion. That is his case against all forms of optimistic rationalism, the natural sciences, liberal theories of progress, German military *expertise*, French sociology, confident social engineering of all kinds. And this is his reason for inventing a Kutuzov who followed his simple, Russian, untutored instinct, and despised or ignored the German, French, and Italian experts; and for raising him to the status of a national hero which he has, partly as a result of Tolstoy's portrait, retained ever since.

'His figures', said Akhsharumov in 1868, immediately on the appearance of the last part of *War and Peace*, 'are real and not mere pawns in the hands of an unintelligible destiny,' the author's theory, on the other hand, was ingenious but irrelevant. This remained the general view of Russian and, for the most part, foreign literary critics too. The Russian left-wing intellectuals attacked Tolstoy for 'social indifferentism', for disparagement of all noble social impulses as a compound of ignorance and foolish monomania, and an 'aristocratic' cynicism about life as a marsh which cannot be reclaimed; Flaubert and Turgenev, as we have seen, thought the tendency to philosophize unfortunate in itself; the only critic who took the doctrine seriously and tried to provide a rational refutation was the historian Kareyev.[1] Patiently and mildly he pointed out that fascinating as the contrast between the reality of personal life and the life of the social ant-hill may be, Tolstoy's conclusions did not follow. True, man is at once an atom living its

[1] N. Kareyev, *Istoricheskaya filosofiya Grafa L. N. Tolstogo* (St. Pbg., 1888); a lecture delivered in April 1886, and first published in *Vestnik Evropy* in 1887.

own conscious life 'for itself', and at the same time the unconscious agent of some historical trend, a relatively insignificant element in the vast whole composed of a very large number of such elements. *War and Peace*, Kareyev tells us, 'is a historical poem on the philosophical theme of duality'—'the two lives lived by men', and Tolstoy was perfectly right to protest that history is not made to happen by the combination of such obscure entities as the 'power' or 'mental activity' assumed by naïve historians; indeed he was, in Kareyev's view, at his best when he denounced the tendency of metaphysically minded writers to attribute causal efficacy to, or idealize, such abstract entities as 'heroes', 'historic forces', 'moral forces', 'nationalism', 'reason' and so on, whereby they simultaneously committed the two deadly sins of inventing non-existent entities to explain concrete events and of giving free reign to personal, or national, or class, or metaphysical bias. So far so good, and Tolstoy is judged to have shown deeper insight—'greater realism'—than most historians. He was right also in demanding that the infinitesimals of history be integrated. But then he himself had done just that by creating the individuals of his novel who are not trivial precisely to the degree to which in their characters and actions, they 'summate' countless others, who between them do 'move history'. This *is* the integrating of infinitesimals, not, of course, by scientific, but by 'artistic-psychological' means. Tolstoy was right to abhor abstractions, but this had led him too far, so that he ended by denying not merely that history was a natural science like chemistry—which was correct—but a science at all, an activity with its own proper concepts and generalizations; which, if true, would abolish all history as such. Tolstoy was right to say that the impersonal 'forces' and 'purposes' of the older historians were myths and dangerously misleading myths, but unless

[33]

we were allowed to ask what made this or that group of individuals—who, in the end, of course, alone were real—behave thus and thus, without needing first to provide separate psychological analyses of each member of the group and then to 'integrate' them all, we could not think about history or society at all. Yet we did do this, and profitably, and to deny that we could discover a good deal by social observation, historical inference and similar means was, for Kareyev, tantamount to denying that we had criteria for distinguishing between historical truth and falsehood which were less or more reliable—and that was surely mere prejudice, fanatical obscurantism. Kareyev declares that it is men, doubtless, who make social forms, but these forms—the ways in which men live—in their turn affect those born into them; individual wills may not be all-powerful, but neither are they totally impotent, and some are more effective than others: Napoleon may not be a demigod, but neither is he a mere epiphenomenon of a process which would have occurred unaltered without him; the 'important people' are less important than they themselves or the more foolish historians may suppose, but neither are they shadows; individuals, besides their intimate inner lives which alone seem real to Tolstoy, have social purposes, and some among them have strong wills too, and these sometimes transform the lives of communities. Tolstoy's notion of inexorable laws which work themselves out whatever men may think or wish is itself an oppressive myth; laws are only statistical probabilities, at any rate in the social sciences, not hideous and inexorable 'forces'—a concept the darkness of which, Kareyev points out, Tolstoy himself in other contexts exposed with such brilliance and malice, when his opponent seemed to him too naïve or too clever or in the grip of some grotesque metaphysic. But to say that unless men make history they are themselves, particularly the 'great' among them, mere 'labels', because history makes itself, and only the unconscious life of the social hive, the human ant-hill, has genuine significance or value and 'reality'——what is this but a wholly unhistorical and dogmatic ethical scepticism? Why should we accept it when empirical evidence points elsewhere?

Kareyev's objections are very reasonable, the most sensible and clearly formulated of all that ever were urged against Tolstoy's view of history. But in a sense he missed the point. Tolstoy was not primarily engaged in exposing the fallacies of histories based on this or that metaphysical schematism, or those which sought to explain too much in terms of some one chosen element particularly dear to the author (all of which Kareyev approves) or to refute the possibility of an empirical science of sociology (which Kareyev thinks unreasonable of him) in order to set up some rival theory of his own. Tolstoy's concern with history derives from a deeper source than abstract interest in historical method or philosophical objections to given types of historical practice. It seems to spring from something more personal, a bitter inner conflict between his actual experience and his beliefs, between his vision of life, and his theory of what it, and he himself, ought to be, if the vision was to be bearable at all; between the immediate data which he was too honest and too intelligent to ignore, and the need for an interpretation of them which did not lead to the childish absurdities of all previous views. For the one conviction to which his temperament and his intellect kept him faithful all his life was that all previous attempts at a rational theodicy—to explain how and why what occurred occurred as and when it did, and why it was bad or good that it should or should not do so—all such efforts were grotesque absurdities, shoddy deceptions which one sharp, honest word was sufficient to blow away. The Russian critic, Boris Eykhenbaum, who has written the best critical work on Tolstoy in any language,[1] in the course of it develops the thesis that what oppressed Tolstoy most was his lack of positive convictions: and that the famous passage in *Anna Karenina* in which Levin's brother tells him that he—Levin—had no positive beliefs, that even communism, with its artificial, 'geometrical', symmetry, is better than total scepticism of his—Levin's—kind, in fact refers to Lev Nikolaevich himself, and to the attacks on him by his brother Nikolai Nikolaevich. Whether or not the passage is literally autobiographical—and there is little in Tolstoy's writing that, in one way or another, is not—Eykhenbaum's theory seems, in general, valid. Tolstoy was by nature not a visionary; he saw the manifold objects and situations on earth in their full multiplicity; he grasped their individual essences, and what divided them from what they were not, with a clarity to which there is no parallel. Any comforting theory which attempted to collect, relate, 'synthesize', reveal hidden substrata and concealed inner connexions, which, though not apparent to the naked eye, nevertheless guaranteed the unity of all things—the fact that they were 'ultimately' parts one of another with no loose ends—the ideal of the seamless whole—all such doctrines he exploded contemptuously and without difficulty. His genius lay in the perception of specific properties, the almost inexpressible individual quality in virtue of which the given object is uniquely different from all others. Nevertheless he longed for a universal explanatory principle; that is the perception of resemblances or common origins, or single purpose, or unity in the apparent variety of the mutually exclusive bits and pieces which

[1] B. Eykhenbaum, *Lev Tolstoy* (vol. i, Leningrad, 1928; vol. ii, Moscow, 1930), i. 123.

composed the furniture of the world.[1] Like all very penetrating, very imaginative, very clear-sighted analysts who dissect or pulverize in order to reach the indestructible core, and justify their own annihilating activities (from which they cannot abstain in any case) by the belief that such a core exists—he continued to kill his rivals' rickety constructions with cold contempt, as being unworthy of intelligent men, always hoping that the desperately-sought-for 'real' unity would presently emerge from the destruction of the shams and frauds—the knock-kneed army of eighteenth- and nineteenth-century philosophies of history. And the more obsessive the suspicion that perhaps the quest was vain, that no core and no unifying principle would ever be discovered, the more ferocious the measures to drive this thought away by increasingly merciless and ingenious executions of more and more false claimants to the title of the truth. As Tolstoy moved away from literature to polemical writing this tendency became increasingly prominent: the irritated awareness at the back of his mind that no final solution was ever, in principle, to be found, caused Tolstoy to attack the bogus solutions all the more savagely for the false comfort they offered—and for being an insult to the intelligence.[2] Tolstoy's purely intellectual genius for this kind of lethal activity was very great and exceptional, and all his life he looked

[1] Here the paradox appears once more; for the 'infinitesimals', whose integration is the task of the ideal historian, must be reasonably uniform to make this operation possible; yet the sense of 'reality' consists in the sense of their unique differences.

[2] In our day French existentialists for similar psychological reasons have struck out against all explanations as such because they are a mere drug to still serious questions, shortlived palliatives for wounds which are unbearable but must be borne, above all not denied or 'explained'; for all explaining is explaining away, and that is a denial of the given—the existent—the brute facts.

for some edifice strong enough to resist his engines of destruction and his mines and battering rams; he wished to be stopped by an immovable obstacle, he wished his violent projectiles to be resisted by impregnable fortifications. The eminent reasonableness and tentative methods of Professor Kareyev, his mild academic remonstrance, were altogether too unlike the final impenetrable, irreducible, solid bed-rock of truth on which alone that secure interpretation of life could be built which all his life he wished to find.

The thin, 'positive' doctrine of historical change in *War and Peace* is all that remains of this despairing search, and it is the immense superiority of Tolstoy's offensive over his defensive weapons that has always made his philosophy of history—the theory of the minute particles, requiring integration—seem so threadbare and artificial to the average, reasonably critical, moderately sensitive reader of the novel. Hence the tendency of most of those who have written about *War and Peace*, both immediately on its appearance and in later years, to maintain Akhsharumov's thesis that Tolstoy's genius lay in his quality as a writer, a creator of a world more real than life itself; while the theoretical disquisitions, even though Tolstoy himself may have looked upon them as the most important ingredient in the book, in fact threw no light either upon the character or the value of the work itself, nor on the creative process by which it was achieved. This anticipated the approach of those psychological critics who maintain that the author himself often scarcely knows the sources of his own activity: that the springs of his genius are invisible to him, the process itself largely unconscious, and his own overt purpose a mere rationalization in his own mind of the true, but scarcely conscious, motives and methods involved in the act of creation, and consequently often a mere hindrance to those dispassionate students of art and literature who are engaged upon the 'scientific'—i.e. naturalistic—analysis of its origins and evolution. Whatever we may think of the general validity of such an outlook, it is something of an historical irony that Tolstoy should have been treated in this fashion; for it is virtually his own way with the academic historians at whom he mocks with such Voltairian irony. And yet there is much poetic justice in it: for the unequal ratio of critical to constructive elements in his own philosophizing seems due to the fact that his sense of reality (a reality which resides in individual persons and their relationships alone) served to explode all the large theories which ignored its findings, but proved insufficient by itself to provide the basis of a more satisfactory general account of the facts. And there is no evidence that Tolstoy himself ever conceived it possible that this was the root of the 'dualism', the failure to reconcile the 'two lives lived by man'.

The unresolved conflict between Tolstoy's belief that the attributes of personal life alone were real and his doctrine that analysis of them is insufficient to explain the course of history (i.e. the behaviour of societies) is paralleled, at a profounder and more personal level, by the conflict between, on the one hand, his own gifts both as a writer and as a man and, on the other, his ideals—that which he sometimes believed himself to be, and at all times profoundly believed in, and wished to be.

If we may recall once again our division of artists into foxes and hedgehogs: Tolstoy perceived reality in its multiplicity, as a collection of separate entities round and into which he saw with a clarity and penetration scarcely ever equalled, but he believed only in on vast, unitary whole. No author who has ever lived has shown such powers of insight into the variety of life—the differences, the contrasts, the collisions of persons and things and situations, each apprehended in its absolute uniqueness and conveyed with a degree of directness and a precision of concrete imagery to be found in no other writer. No one has ever excelled Tolstoy in expressing the specific flavour, the exact quality of a feeling—the degree of its 'oscillation', the ebb and flow, the minute movements (which Turgenev mocked as a mere trick on his part)—the inner and outer texture and 'feel' of a look, a thought, a pang of sentiment, no less than that of the specific pattern of a situation, or an entire period, continuous segments of lives of individuals, families, communities, entire nations. The celebrated life-likeness of every object and every person in his world derives from this astonishing capacity of presenting every ingredient of it in its fullest individual essence, in all its many dimensions, as it were; never as a mere datum, however vivid, within some stream of consciousness, with blurred edges, an outline, a shadow, an impressionistic representation: nor yet calling for, and dependent on, some process of reasoning in the mind of the reader; but always as a solid object, seen simultaneously from near and far, in natural, unaltering daylight, from all possible angles of vision, set in an absolutely specific context in time and space—an event fully present to the senses or the imagination in all its facets, with every nuance sharply and firmly articulated.

Yet what he believed in was the opposite. He advocated a single embracing vision; he preached not variety but simplicity, not many levels of consciousness but reduction to some single level—in *War and Peace* to the standard of the good man, the single, spontaneous, open soul: as later to that of the peasants, or of a simple Christian ethic divorced from any complex theology or metaphysic, some simple, quasi-utilitarian criterion, whereby everything is interrelated directly, and all the items can be assessed in terms of one another by some simple measuring rod. Tolstoy's genius lies in a capacity for marvellously accurate reproduction of the irreproducible, the almost miraculous evocation of the full, untranslatable individuality of the individual, which induces in the reader an acute awareness of the presence of the object itself, and not of a mere description of it, employing for this purpose metaphors which fix the quality of a particular experience as such, and avoiding those general terms which relate it to similar instances by ignoring individual differences—'the oscillations of feeling'—in favour of what is common to them all. But then this same writer pleads for, indeed preaches with great fury, particularly in his last, religious phase, the exact opposite: the necessity of expelling everything that does not submit to some very general, very simple standard: say, what peasants like or dislike, or what the gospels declare to be good.

This violent contradiction between the data of experience from which he could not liberate himself, and which, of course, all his life he knew alone to be real, and his deeply metaphysical belief in the existence of a system to which they *must* belong, whether they appear to do so or not, this conflict between instinctive judgment and theoretical conviction— between his gifts and his opinions—mirrors the unresolved conflict between the reality of the moral life with its sense of responsibility, joys, sorrows, sense of guilt and sense of achievement—all of which is nevertheless illusion; and the laws which govern everything, although we cannot know more than a negligible portion of them—so that all scientists and historians who say that they do know them and are guided by them are lying and deceiving—but which nevertheless alone are real. Beside Tolstoy, Gogol' and Dostoevsky, whose abnormality is so often contrasted with Tolstoy's 'sanity', are well-integrated personalities, with a coherent outlook and a single vision. Yet out of this violent conflict grew *War and Peace*: its marvellous solidity should not blind us to the deep cleavage which yawns open whenever Tolstoy remembers, or rather reminds himself—fails to forget—what he is doing, and why.

IV

Theories are seldom born in the void. And the question of the roots of Tolstoy's vision of history is therefore a reasonable one. Everything that Tolstoy writes on history has a stamp of his own original personality, a first-hand quality denied to most writers on abstract topics. On these subjects he wrote as an amateur, not as a professional; but let it be remembered that he belonged to the world of great affairs: he was a member of the ruling class of his country and his time, and knew and understood it completely; he lived in an environment exceptionally crowded with theories and ideas, he examined a great deal of material for *War and Peace* (though, as several Russian scholars have shown,[1] not as much as is sometimes supposed), he travelled a great deal, and met many notable public figures in Germany and France.

That he read widely, and was influenced by what he read, cannot be doubted. It is a commonplace that he owed a great deal to Rousseau, and probably derived from him, as much as from Diderot and the French Enlightenment, his analytic, anti-historical way of approaching social problems, in particular the tendency to treat them in terms of timeless, logical, moral, and metaphysical categories, and not look for their essence, as the German historical school advocated, in terms of growth, and of response to a changing historical environment. He remained an admirer

[1] e.g. by both Shklovsky and Eykhenbaum in the works cited above.

of Rousseau, and late in life still recommended *Émile* as the best book ever written on education.[1] Rousseau must have strengthened, if he did not actually originate, his growing tendency to idealize the soil and its cultivators—the simple peasant, who for Tolstoy is a repository of almost as rich a stock of 'natural' virtues as Rousseau's noble savage. Rousseau, too, must have reinforced the coarse-grained, rough peasant in Tolstoy with his strongly moralistic, puritanical strain, his suspicion of, and antipathy to the rich, the powerful, the happy as such, his streak of genuine vandalism, and occasional bursts of blind, very Russian rage against Western sophistication and refinement, and that adulation of 'virtue' and simple tastes, of the 'healthy' moral life, the militant, anti-liberal barbarism, which is one of Rousseau's specific contributions to the stock of Jacobin ideas. And perhaps Rousseau influenced him also in setting so high a value upon family life, and in his doctrine of superiority of the heart over the head, of moral over intellectual or aesthetic virtues. This has been noted before, and it is true and illuminating, but it does not account for Tolstoy's theory of history of which little trace can be found in the profoundly unhistorical Rousseau. Indeed in so far as Rousseau seeks to derive the right of some men to authority over others from a theory of the transference of power in accordance with the Social Contract, Tolstoy contemptuously refutes him.

We get somewhat nearer to the truth if we consider the influence upon Tolstoy of his romantic and conservative Slavophil contemporaries. He was close to some among them, particularly to Pogodin and Samarin, in the mid-sixties when he was writing *War*

[1] 'On n'a pas rendu justice à Rousseau . . . J'ai lu tout Rousseau, oui, tous les vingt volumes, y compris le *Dictionnaire de musique*. Je faisais mieux que l'admirer; je lui rendais une culte véritable . . .' see p. 47, note 1.

and Peace, and certainly shared their antagonism to the scientific theories of history then fashionable, whether to the metaphysical positivism of Comte and his followers, or the more materialistic views of Chernyshevsky and Pisarev, as well as those of Buckle and Mill and Herbert Spencer, and the general British empiricist tradition, tinged by French and German scientific materialism, to which these very different figures all, in their various fashions, belonged. The Slavophils (and perhaps especially Tyutchev, whose poetry Tolstoy admired so deeply) may have done something to discredit for him historical theories modelled upon the natural sciences, which, for Tolstoy no less than for Dostoevsky, failed to give a true account of what men did and suffered. They were inadequate if only because they ignored man's 'inner' experience, treated him as a natural object played upon by the same forces as all the other constituents of the material world, and taking the French Encyclopaedists at their word, tried to study social behaviour as one might study a beehive or an ant-hill, and then complained because the laws which they formulated failed to explain the behaviour of living men and women. These romantic medievalists may moreover have strengthened Tolstoy's natural anti-intellectualism and anti-liberalism, and his deeply sceptical and pessimistic view of the strength of non-rational motives in human behaviour, which at once dominate human beings and deceive them about themselves—in short that innate conservatism of outlook which very early made Tolstoy deeply suspect to the radical Russian intelligentsia of the fifties and sixties, and led them to think of him uneasily as being after all a count, an officer and a reactionary, not one of themselves, not genuinely enlightened or *révolté* at all, despite his boldest protests against the political system, his heterodoxies, his destructive nihilism.

But although Tolstoy and the Slavophils may have fought a common enemy, their positive views diverged sharply. The Slavophil doctrine derived principally from German Idealism, in particular from Schelling's view, despite much lip-service to Hegel and his interpreters, that true knowledge could not be obtained by the use of reason, but only by a kind of imaginative self-identification with the central principle of the universe—the soul of the world, such as artists and thinkers have in moments of divine inspiration. Some of the Slavophils identified this with the revealed truths of the orthodox religion and the mystical tradition of the Russian Church, and bequeathed it to the Russian symbolist poets and philosophers of a later generation. Tolstoy stood at the opposite pole to all this. He believed that only by patient empirical observation could any knowledge be obtained; that this knowledge is always inadequate, that simple people often know the truth better than learned men, because their observation of men and nature -is less clouded by empty theories, and not because they are inspired vehicles of the divine afflatus. There is a hard cutting edge of common sense about everything that Tolstoy wrote which automatically puts to flight metaphysical fantasies and undisciplined tendencies towards esoteric experience, or the poetical or theological interpretations of life, which lay at the heart of the Slavophil outlook, and (as in the analogous case of the anti-industrial romanticism of the West), determined both its hatred of politics and economics in the ordinary sense, and its mystical nationalism. Moreover, the Slavophils were worshippers of historical method as alone disclosing the true nature—revealed only in its impalpable growth in time—of individual institutions and abstract sciences alike. None of this could possibly have found a sympathetic echo in the very tough-minded, very matter of fact Tolstoy, especially the realistic Tolstoy of the middle years; if the peasant Platon Karataev has something in common with the agrarian *ethos* of the Slavophil (and indeed Pan-Slav) ideologists—simple rural wisdom as against the absurdities of the over-clever West—yet Pierre Bezukhov in the early drafts of *War and Peace* ends his life as a Decembrist and an exile in Siberia, and cannot be conceived in all his spiritual wanderings as ultimately finding comfort in any metaphysical system, still less in the bosom of the Orthodox, or any other, established, Church. The Slavophils saw through the pretensions of Western social and psychological science, and that was sympathetic to Tolstoy; but their positive doctrines interested him little. He was against unintelligible mysteries, against mists of antiquity, against any kind of recourse to mumbo-jumbo: his hostile picture of the freemasons in *War and Peace* remained symptomatic of his attitude to the end. This can only have been reinforced by his interest in the writings of, and his visit in 1861 to, the exiled Proudhon, whose confused irrationalism, puritanism, hatred of authority and *bourgeois* intellectuals, and general Rousseauism and violence of tone evidently pleased him. It is more than possible that he took the title of his novel from Proudhon's *La Guerre et la Paix* published in the same year.

If the classical German idealists had had no direct effect upon Tolstoy, there was at least one German philosopher for whom he did express admiration. And indeed it is not difficult to see why he found Schopenhauer attractive; that solitary thinker drew a gloomy picture of the impotent human will beating desperately against the rigidly determined laws of the universe; he spoke of the vanity of all human passions, the absurdity of rational systems, the universal failure to understand the non-rational springs of action and feeling, the suffering to which all flesh is subject, and

[46]

the consequent desirability of reducing human vulnerability by reducing man himself to the condition of the utmost quietism, where, being passionless, he cannot be frustrated or humiliated or wounded. This celebrated doctrine reflected Tolstoy's later views—that man suffers much because he seeks too much, is foolishly ambitious and grotesquely over-estimates his capacities; from Schopenhauer, too, may come the bitter emphasis laid on the familiar contrast of the illusion of free will with the reality of the iron laws which govern the world, in particular the account of the inevitable suffering which this illusion, since it cannot be made to vanish, must inevitably cause. This, for both Schopenhauer and Tolstoy, is the central tragedy of human life; if only men would learn how little the cleverest and most gifted among them can control, how little they can know of all the multitude of factors the orderly movement of which is the history of the world; above all, what presumptuous nonsense it is to claim to perceive an order merely on the strength of believing desperately that an order must exist, when all one actually perceives is meaningless chaos—a chaos of which the heightened form, the microcosm in which the disorder of human life is reflected in an intense degree, is war.

The best avowed of all Tolstoy's literary debts is, of course, that to Stendhal. In his celebrated interview in 1901 with M. Paul Boyer,[1] Tolstoy coupled Stendhal with Rousseau as the two writers to whom he owed most, and added that all he had learnt about war he had learnt from Stendhal's description of the battle of Waterloo in *La Chartreuse de Parme*, where Fabrice wanders about the battlefield 'understanding nothing'. And he added that this conception—war 'without *panache*' or 'embellishments', of which his brother

[1] See *Paul Boyer chez Tolstoï* (Paris, 1950), p. 40.

Nikolai had spoken to him, he later had verified for himself during his own service in the Crimean War. Nothing ever won so much praise from active soldiers as Tolstoy's *vignettes* of episodes in the war, his descriptions of how battles appear to those who are actually engaged in them. No doubt Tolstoy was right in declaring that he owed much of this dry light to Stendhal. But there is a figure behind Stendhal even drier, even more destructive, from whom Stendhal may well, at least in part, have derived his new method of interpreting social life, a celebrated writer with whose works Tolstoy was certainly acquainted and to whom he owed a deeper debt than is commonly supposed; for the striking resemblance between their views can hardly be put down either to accident, or the mysterious operations of the *Zeitgeist*. This figure was the famous Joseph de Maistre; and the full story of his influence on Tolstoy, although it has been noted by students of Tolstoy, and by at least one critic of Maistre,[1] still largely remains to be written.

V

On 1 November 1865, in the middle of writing *War and Peace*, Tolstoy wrote down in his diary 'I am reading Maistre',[2] and on 7 September 1866 he wrote to the editor Bartenev, who acted as a kind of general assistant to him, asking him to send the 'Maistre archive', i.e. his letters and notes. There is every reason why Tolstoy should have read this now relatively little read author. Count Joseph de Maistre was a Savoyard royalist who had first made a name for himself by writing anti-revolutionary tracts during

[1] See Adolfo Omodeo, *Un Reazionario* (Bari: Laterza, 1939), p. 112, note 1.

[2] 'Chitayu "Maistre"', quoted by B. Eykhenbaum, op. cit., ii. 309–17.

the last years of the eighteenth century. Although normally classified as an orthodox Catholic reactionary writer, a pillar of the Bourbon Restoration and a defender of the pre-revolutionary *status quo*, in particular of papal authority, he was a great deal more than this. He held grimly unconventional and misanthropic views about the nature of individuals and societies, and wrote with a dry and ironical violence about the incurably savage and wicked nature of man, the inevitability of perpetual slaughter, the divinely instituted character of wars, and the overwhelming part played in human affairs by the passion for self-immolation which, more than natural sociability or artificial agreements, creates armies and civil societies alike; he emphasized the need for absolute authority, punishment and continual repression if civilization and order were to survive at all. Both the content and the tone of his writing are closer to Nietzsche, D'Annunzio, and the heralds of modern fascism than to the respectable royalists of his own time, and caused a stir in their own day both among the legitimists and in Napoleonic France. In 1803 Maistre was sent by his master, the King of Savoy, then living in exile in Rome as a victim of Napoleon and soon forced to move to Sardinia, as his semi-official representative to the Court of St. Petersburg. Maistre, who possessed considerable social charm as well as an acute sense of his environment, made a great impression upon the society of the Russian capital as a polished courtier, a wit and a shrewd political observer. He remained in St. Petersburg from 1803 to 1817, and his exquisitely written and often uncannily penetrating and prophetic diplomatic dispatches and letters, as well as his private correspondence and the various scattered notes on Russia and her inhabitants, sent to his government as well as to his friends and consultants among the Russian nobility, form a uniquely valuable source of information about the life and opinions of the ruling circles of the Russian Empire during and immediately after the Napoleonic period.

He died in 1821, the author of several theologico-political essays, but the definitive edition of his works, in particular of the celebrated *Soirées de St. Pétersbourg*, which in the form of Platonic dialogue dealt with the nature and sanctions of human government and other political and philosophical problems, as well as his *Correspondance diplomatique* and his letters, was published in full only in the fifties and early sixties by his son Rodolphe and by others. Maistre's open hatred of Austria, his anti-Bonapartism, as well as the rising importance of the Piedmontese kingdom before and after the Crimean War, naturally increased interest in his personality and his thought at this date. Books on him began to appear and excited a good deal of discussion in Russian literary and historical circles. Tolstoy possessed the *Soirées*, as well as Maistre's diplomatic correspondence and letters, and copies of them were to be found in the library at Yasnaya Polyana. It is in any case quite clear that Tolstoy used them extensively in *War and Peace*.[1] Thus the celebrated description of Paulucci's intervention in the debate of the Russian General Staff at Drissa is reproduced almost verbatim from a letter by Maistre. Similarly Prince Vassili's conversation at Mme Scherer's reception with the 'homme de beaucoup de mérite' about Kutuzov, is obviously based on a letter by Maistre, in which all the French phrases with which this conversation is sprinkled are to be found. There is, moreover, a note in one of Tolstoy's early rough drafts, 'at Anna Pavlovna's Maistre—Vicomte', which refers to the *raconteur* who tells the beautiful Hélène and an admiring circle of listeners the idiotic anecdote about the

[1] See Eykhenbaum, op. cit.

meeting of Napoleon with the Duc d'Enghien at supper with the celebrated actress Mlle Georges. Again old Prince Bolkonsky's habit of shifting his bed from one room to another is probably taken from a story which Maistre tells about the similar habit of Count Stroganov. Finally the name of Maistre occurs in the novel itself, as being among those who agree that it would be embarrassing and senseless to capture the more eminent princes and marshals of Napoleon's army, since this would merely create diplomatic difficulties. Zhikharev, whose memoirs Tolstoy is known to have used, met Maistre in 1807, and described him in glowing colours;[1] something of the atmosphere to be found in these memoirs enters into Tolstoy's description of the eminent *émigrés* in Anna Pavlovna Scherer's drawing-room, with which *War and Peace* opens, and his other references to fashionable Petersburg society at this date. These echoes and parallels have been collated carefully by Tolstoyan scholars, and leave no doubt about the extent of Tolstoy's borrowing.

Among these parallels there are similarities of a more important kind. Maistre explains that the victory of the legendary Horatius over the Curiatii—like all victories in general—was due to the intangible factor of morale, and Tolstoy similarly speaks of the supreme importance of this unknown quantity in determining the outcome of battles—the impalpable 'spirit' of troops and their commanders. This emphasis on the imponderable and the incalculable is part and parcel of Maistre's general irrationalism. More clearly and boldly than anyone before him Maistre declared that the human intellect was but a feeble instrument when pitted against the power of natural forces; that rational explanations of human conduct seldom explained anything. He maintained that only

[1] S. P. Zhikharev, *Zapiski* (Akademiya), ii. 112–13.

the irrational, precisely because it defied explanation and could therefore not be undermined by the critical activities of reason, was able to persist and be strong. And he gave as examples such irrational institutions as hereditary monarchy and marriage, which survived from age to age, while such rational institutions as elective monarchy, or 'free' personal relationships, swiftly and for no obvious 'reason' collapsed wherever they were introduced. Maistre conceived of life as a savage battle at all levels, between plants and animals no less than individuals and nations, a battle from which no gain was expected, but which originated in some primal, mysterious, sanguinary, self-immolatory craving implanted by God. This instinct was far more powerful than the feeble efforts of rational men who tried to achieve peace and happiness (which was, in any case, not the deepest desire of the human heart— only of its caricature, the liberal intellect) by planning the life of society without reckoning with the violent forces which sooner or later would inevitably cause their puny structures to collapse like so many houses of cards. Maistre regarded the battlefield as typical of life in all its aspects, and derided the generals who thought that they were in fact controlling the movements of their troops and directing the course of the battle. He declared that no one in the actual heat of battle can begin to tell what is going on:

'On parle beaucoup de batailles dans le monde sans savoir ce que c'est; on est surtout assez sujet à les considérer comme des points, tandis qu'elles couvrent deux ou trois lieues de pays; on vous dit gravement: Comment ne savez-vous pas ce qui s'est passé dans ce combat puisque vous y étiez? tandis que c'est précisément le contraire qu'on pourrait dire assez souvent. Celui qui est à la droite sait-il ce qui se passe à la gauche? sait-il seulement ce qui se passe à deux pas de lui? Je me représente aisément une de ces scènes épouvantables: sur un vaste terrain couvert de tous les apprêts du carnage, et qui semble s'ébranler sous les pas des hommes et des chevaux; au milieu du feu et des tourbillons de fumée; étourdi, transporté par le retentissement des armes à feu et des instruments militaires, par des voix qui commandent, qui hurlent ou qui s'éteignent; environné de morts, de mourants, de cadavres mutilés; possédé tour à tour par la crainte, par l'espérance, par la rage, par cinq ou six ivresses différentes, que devient l'homme? que voit-il? que sait-il au bout de quelques heures? que peut-il sur lui et sur les autres? Parmi cette foule de guerriers qui ont combattu tout le jour, il n'y en a souvent pas un seul, et pas même le général, qui sache où est le vainqueur. Il ne tiendrait qu'à moi de vous citer des batailles modernes, des batailles fameuses dont la mémoire ne périra jamais; des batailles qui ont changé la face des affaires en Europe, et qui n'ont été perdues que parce que tel ou tel homme a cru qu'elles l'étaient; de manière qu'en supposant toutes les circonstances égales, et pas une goutte de sang de plus versée de part et d'autre, un autre général aurait fait chanter le *Te Deum* chez lui, et forcé l'histoire de dire tout le contraire de ce qu'elle dira.'[1]

And later:

'N'avons-nous pas fini même par voir perdre des batailles gagnées? . . . Je crois en général que les batailles ne se gagnent ni ne se perdent point physiquement.'[2]

And again, in a similar strain:

'De même une armée de 40,000 hommes est inférieure physiquement à une autre armée de 60,000: mais si la première a plus de courage, d'expérience et de discipline, elle pourra battre la seconde; car elle a plus d'action avec moins de masse, et c'est ce nous voyons à chaque page de l'histoire.[3]

[1] J. de Maistre, *Les Soirées de St. Pétersbourg* (sixième édition, Paris, 1850), tome ii, Entretien vii, pp. 44–5.

[2] Ibid., p. 46.

[3] Ibid., p. 37. The last sentence is reproduced by Tolstoy almost verbatim.

And finally:

'C'est l'opinion qui perd les batailles, et c'est l'opinion qui les gagne.'[1]

Victory is a moral or psychological, not a physical issue:

'Qu'est ce qu'une bataille perdue? . . . *C'est une bataille qu'on croit avoir perdue.* Rien n'est plus vrai. Un homme qui se bat avec un autre est vaincu lorsqu'il est tué ou terrassé, et que l'autre est debout; il n'en est pas ainsi de deux armées: l'une ne peut être tuée, tandis que l'autre reste en pied. Les forces se balancent ainsi que les morts, et depuis surtout que l'invention de la poudre a mis plus d'égalité dans les moyens de destruction, une bataille ne se perd plus matériellement; c'est-à-dire parce qu'il y a plus de morts d'un côté que de l'autre: aussi Frédéric II, qui s'y entendait un peu, disait: *Vaincre, c'est avancer.* Mais quel est celui qui avance? c'est celui dont la conscience et la contenance font reculer l'autre.'[2]

There is and can be no military science, for 'C'est l'imagination qui perd les batailles',[3] and 'peu de batailles sont perdues physiquement—vous tirez, je tire . . . le véritable vainqueur, comme le véritable vaincu, c'est celui qui croit l'être'.[4]

This is the lesson which Tolstoy says he derives from Stendhal, but the words of Prince Andrey about Austerlitz—'We lost because we told ourselves we lost'—as well as the attribution of Russian victory over Napoleon to the strength of the Russian desire to survive, echo Maistre and not Stendhal.

This close parallelism between Maistre's and Tolstoy's views about the chaos and uncontrollability of battles and wars, with its larger implications for human life generally, together with the contempt of both for

[1] Ibid., p. 40.
[2] Ibid., p. 41.
[3] Ibid., p. 43.
[4] Letters, 14 September 1812.

the naïve explanations provided by academic historians to account for human violence and lust for war, was noted by the eminent French historian Albert Sorel, in a little-known lecture to the École des Sciences Politiques delivered on 7 April 1888.[1] He drew a parallel between Maistre and Tolstoy, and observed that although Maistre was a theocrat, while Tolstoy was a 'nihilist', yet both regarded the first causes of events as mysterious, involving the reduction of human wills to nullity. 'The distance', wrote Sorel, 'from the theocrat to the mystic, and from the mystic to the nihilist, is smaller than that from the butterfly to the larva, from the larva to the chrysalis, from the chrysalis to the butterfly.' Tolstoy resembles Maistre in being, above all, curious about first causes, in asking such questions as Maistre's 'Expliquez pourquoi ce qu'il y a de plus honorable dans le monde, au jugement de tout le genre humain sans exception, est le droit de verser innocemment le sang innocent?',[2] in rejecting all rationalist or naturalistic answers, in stressing impalpable psychological and 'spiritual'— and sometimes 'zoological'—factors as determining events, and in stressing these at the expense of statistical analyses of military strength, very much like Maistre in his dispatches to his government at Cagliari. Indeed, Tolstoy's accounts of mass movements—in battle, and in the flight of the Russians from Moscow

[1] A. Sorel, 'Tolstoï—historien', in *Revue Bleue* (Paris) 1888, pp. 460–599. This lecture, which is not reprinted in Sorel's collected works, has been unjustly neglected by students of Tolstoy; it does much to correct the views of those (e.g. P. I. Biryukov and K. Pokrovsky in their works cited above, not to mention later critics and literary historians who almost all rely upon their authority) who omit all reference to Maistre. E. Haumant is almost unique among earlier scholars in ignoring secondary authorities, and discovering the truth for himself; see his *La Culture Française en Russie* (Paris, 1910), pp. 490–2.

[2] *Soirées*, Entretien, vii, p. 13.

or of the French from Russia—might almost be designed to give concrete illustrations of Maistre's theory of the unplanned and unplannable character of all great events. But the parallel runs deeper. The Savoyard Count and the Russian are both reacting, and reacting violently, against liberal optimism concerning human goodness, human reason, and the value or inevitability of material progress: both furiously denounce the notion that mankind can be made eternally happy and virtuous by rational and scientific means.

The first great wave of optimistic rationalism which followed the Wars of Religion broke against the violence of the great French Revolution and the political despotism and social and economic misery which ensued: in Russia a similar development was shattered by the long succession of repressive measures taken by Nicholas I to counteract firstly the effect of the Decembrist revolt, and, nearly a quarter of a century later, the influence of the European Revolutions of 1848–9; and to this must be added the material and moral effect, a decade later, of the Crimean *débâcle*. In both cases the emergence of naked force killed a great deal of tender-minded idealism, and resulted in various types of realism and toughness—among others, of materialistic socialism, authoritarian neo-feudalism, blood-and-iron nationalism and other bitterly anti-liberal movements. In the case of both Maistre and Tolstoy, for all their unbridgeably deep psychological, social, cultural, and religious differences, the disillusionment took the form of an acute scepticism about scientific method as such, distrust of all liberalism, positivism, rationalism, and of all the forms of high-minded secularism then influential in western Europe; and led to a deliberate emphasis on the 'unpleasant' aspects of human history, from which sentimental romantics, humanist historians, and optimistic social theorists seemed so resolutely to be averting their gaze.

Both Maistre and Tolstoy spoke of political reformers (in one interesting instance, of the same individual representative of it, the Russian statesman Speransky) in the same tone of bitterly contemptuous irony. Maistre was suspected of having had an actual hand in Speransky's fall and exile; Tolstoy, through the eyes of Prince Andrey, describes the pale face of Alexander's one-time favourite, his soft hands, his fussy and self-important manner, the artificiality and emptiness of his movements—as somehow indicative of unreality of his person and of his liberal activities—in a manner which Maistre could only have applauded. Both speak of intellectuals with scorn and hostility. Maistre regards them as being not merely grotesque casualties of the historical process—hideous cautions created by Providence to scare mankind into return to the ancient Roman faith—but as beings dangerous to society, a pestilential sect of questioners and corrupters of youth against whose corrosive activity all prudent rulers must take measures. Tolstoy treats them with contempt rather than hatred, and represents them as poor, misguided, feeble-witted creatures with delusions of grandeur. Maistre sees them as a brood of social and political locusts, as a canker at the heart of Christian civilization which is of all things the most sacred and will be preserved only by the heroic efforts of the Pope and his Church. Tolstoy looks on them as clever fools, spinners of empty subtleties, blind and deaf to the realities which simpler hearts can grasp, and from time to time he lets fly at them with the brutal violence of a grim, anarchical old peasant, avenging himself, after years of silence, on the silly, chattering, town-bred monkeys, so knowing, and full of words to explain everything, and superior, and impotent and empty.

Both dismiss any interpretation of history which does not place at the heart of it the problem of the nature of power, and both speak with disdain about rationalistic attempts to explain it. Maistre amuses himself at the expense of the Encyclopaedists—their clever superficialities, their neat but empty categories—very much in the manner adopted by Tolstoy towards their descendants a century later—the scientific sociologists and historians. Both profess belief in the deep wisdom of the uncorrupted common people, although Maistre's mordant *obiter dicta* about the hopeless barbarism, venality and ignorance of the Russians cannot have been to Tolstoy's taste, if indeed he ever read them.

Both Maistre and Tolstoy regard the Western world as in some sense 'rotting', as being in rapid decay. This was the doctrine which the Roman Catholic counter-revolutionaries at the turn of the century virtually invented, and it formed part of their view of the French Revolution as a divine punishment visited upon those who strayed from the Christian faith and in particular that of the Roman Church. From France this denunciation of secularism was carried by many devious routes, mainly by second-rate journalists and their academic readers, to Germany and to Russia (to Russia both directly and via German versions), where it found a ready soil among those who, having themselves avoided the revolutionary upheavals, found it flattering to their *amour-propre* to believe that they, at any rate, might still be on the path to greater power and glory, while the West, destroyed by the failure of its ancient faith, was fast disintegrating morally and politically. No doubt Tolstoy derived this element in his outlook at least as much from Slavophils and other Russian chauvinists as directly from Maistre, but it is worth noting that this belief is exceptionally powerful in both these dry and aristocratic observers, and governs their oddly similar outlooks. Both were *au fond* unyieldingly pessimistic thinkers, whose ruthless destruction of current illusions frightened off their contemporaries even when they reluctantly conceded the truth of what was said. Despite the fact that Maistre was fanatically ultramontane and a supporter of established institutions, while Tolstoy, unpolitical in his earlier work, gave no evidence of radical sentiment, both were obscurely felt to be nihilistic—the humane values of the nineteenth century fell to pieces under their fingers. Both sought for some escape from their own inescapable and unanswerable scepticism in some vast, impregnable truth which would protect them from the effects of their own natural inclinations and temperament: Maistre in the Church, Tolstoy in the uncorrupted human heart and simple brotherly love —a state he could have known but seldom, an ideal before the vision of which all his descriptive skill deserts him and usually yields something inartistic, wooden and naïve; painfully touching, painfully unconvincing, and conspicuously remote from his own experience.

Yet the analogy must not be overstressed: it is true that both Maistre and Tolstoy attach the greatest possible importance to war and conflict, but Maistre, like Proudhon after him,[1] glorifies war, and declares

[1] Tolstoy visited Proudhon in Brussels in 1861, the year in which the latter published a work which was called *La Guerre et la Paix*, translated into Russian three years later. On the basis of this fact Eykhenbaum tries to deduce the influence of Proudhon upon Tolstoy's novel. Proudhon follows Maistre in regarding the origins of wars as a dark and sacred mystery; and there is much confused irrationalism, puritanism, love of paradox, and general Rousseauism in all his work. But these qualities are widespread in radical French thought, and it is difficult to find anything specifically Proudhonist in Tolstoy's *War and Peace*, besides the title. The extent of Proudhon's general influence on all kinds of Russian intellectuals during this period was, of course, very large; it would thus be just as easy, indeed easier, to construct a case for

it to be mysterious and divine, while Tolstoy detests
it and regards it as in principle explicable if only we
knew enough of the many minute causes—the celebrated 'differential' of history. Maistre believed in
authority because it was an irrational force, he believed
in the need to submit, in the inevitability of crime and
the supreme importance of inquisitions and punishment. He regarded the executioner as the corner-stone
of society, and it was not for nothing that Stendhal
called him *L'ami du bourreau* and Lamennais said of
him that there were only two realities for him—crime
and punishment—'his works are as though written
on the scaffold'. Maistre's vision of the world is one
of savage creatures tearing each other limb from limb,
killing for the sake of killing, with violence and blood,
which he sees as the normal condition of all animate
life. Tolstoy is far from such horror, crime, and
sadism:[1] and he is not, *pace* Albert Sorel and Vogüé, in
any sense a mystic: he has no fear of questioning anything, and believes that some simple answer must exist
—if only we did not insist on tormenting ourselves
with searching for it in strange and remote places,
when it lies all the time at our feet. Maistre supported
the principle of hierarchy and believed in a self-
sacrificing aristocracy, heroism, obedience, and the
most rigid control of the masses by their social and
theological superiors. Accordingly, he advocated that
education in Russia be placed in the hands of the

regarding Dostoevsky—or Maxim Gorky—as a *Proudhonisant* as to
look on Tolstoy as one; yet this would be no more than an idle
exercise in critical ingenuity; for the resemblances are vague and
general, while the differences are deeper, more numerous and
more specific.

[1] Yet Tolstoy, too, says that millions of men kill each other,
knowing that it is physically and morally evil, because it is
'necessary'; because in doing so, men 'fulfilled ... an elemental,
zoological law'. This is pure Maistre, and very remote from
Stendhal or Rousseau.

[60]

Jesuits; they would at least inculcate into the barbarous Scythians the Latin language which was the sacred tongue of humanity if only because it embodied the prejudices and superstitions of previous ages—beliefs which had stood the test of history and experience—alone able to form a wall strong enough to keep out the terrible acids of atheism, liberalism, and freedom of thought. Above all he regarded natural science and secular literature as dangerous commodities in the hands of those not completely indoctrinated against them, a heady wine which would dangerously excite, and in the end destroy, any society not used to it.

Tolstoy all his life fought against open obscurantism and artificial repression of the desire for knowledge; his harshest words were directed against those Russian statesmen and publicists in the last quarter of the nineteenth century—Pobyedonostsev and his friends and minions—who practised precisely these maxims of the great Catholic reactionary. The author of *War and Peace* plainly hated the Jesuits, and particularly detested their success in converting Russian ladies of fashion during Alexander's reign—the final events in the life of Pierre's worthless wife, Hélène, might almost have been founded upon Maistre's activities as a missionary to the aristocracy of St. Petersburg: indeed, there is every reason to think that the Jesuits were expelled from Russia, and Maistre himself was virtually recalled, when his interference was deemed too overt and too successful by the Emperor himself.

Nothing, therefore, would have shocked and irritated Tolstoy so much as to be told that he had a great deal in common with this apostle of darkness, this defender of ignorance and serfdom. Nevertheless, of all writers on social questions, Maistre's tone most nearly resembles that of Tolstoy. Both preserve the same sardonic, almost cynical, disbelief in the improvement of society by rational means, by the enactment of good laws or the propagation of scientific knowledge. Both speak with the same angry irony of every fashionable explanation, every social nostrum, particularly of the ordering and planning of society in accordance with some man-made formula. In Maistre openly, and in Tolstoy less obviously, there is a deeply sceptical attitude towards all experts and all techniques, all high-minded professions of secular faith and and efforts at social improvement by well-meaning but, alas, idealistic persons; there is the same distaste for anyone who deals in ideas, who believes in abstract principles: and both are deeply affected by Voltaire's temper, and bitterly reject his views. Both ultimately appeal to some elemental source concealed in the souls of men, Maistre even while denouncing Rousseau as a false prophet, Tolstoy with his more ambiguous attitude towards him. Both above all reject the concept of individual political liberty: of civil rights guaranteed by some impersonal system of justice. Maistre, because he regarded any desire for personal freedom—whether political or economic or social or cultural or religious—as wilful indiscipline and stupid insubordination, and supported tradition in its most darkly irrational and repressive forms, because it alone provided the energy which gave life, continuity, and safe anchorage to social institutions; Tolstoy rejected political reform because he believed that ultimate regeneration could come only from within, and that the inner life was only lived truly in the untouched depths of the mass of the people.

VI

But there is a larger and more important parallel between Tolstoy's interpretation of history and the ideas of Maistre, and it raises issues of fundamental principle concerning knowledge of the past. One of the most striking elements common to the thought of these dissimilar, and indeed antagonistic, *penseurs*, is their preoccupation with the 'inexorable' character— the 'march'—of events. Both Tolstoy and Maistre think of what occurs as a thick, opaque, inextricably complex web of events, objects, characteristics, connected and divided by literally innumerable unidentifiable links—and gaps and sudden discontinuities too, visible and invisible. It is a view of reality which makes all clear, logical and scientific constructions— the well defined, symmetrical patterns of human reason—seem smooth, thin, empty, 'abstract' and totally ineffective as means either of description or of analysis of anything that lives, or has ever lived. Maistre attributes this to the incurable impotence of human powers of observation and of reasoning, at least when they function without the aid of the superhuman sources of knowledge—faith, revelation, tradition, above all the mystical vision of the great saints and doctors of the Church, their unanalysable, special sense of reality to which natural science, free criticism and the secular spirit are fatal. The wisest of the Greeks, many among the great Romans, and after them the dominant ecclesiastics and statesmen of the Middle Ages, Maistre tells us, possessed this insight; from it flowed their power, their dignity and their success. The natural enemies of this spirit are cleverness and specialization: hence the contempt so rightly shown for, in the Roman world, experts and technicians—the *Graeculus esuriens*—the remote but unmistakable ancestors of the sharp, wizened figures of the modern Alexandrian Age—the terrible Eighteenth Century—all the *écrivasserie et avocasserie*—the miserable crew of scribblers and attorneys, with the predatory, sordid, grinning figure of Voltaire at their head, destructive and self-destructive, because blind and deaf to the true Word of God. Only the Church understands the 'inner' rhythms, the 'deeper' currents of the world, the silent march of things; *non in commotione Dominus;* not in noisy democratic manifestoes nor in the rattle of constitutional formulae, nor in revolutionary violence, but in the eternal natural order, governed by 'Natural' law. Only those who understand it, know what can and what cannot be achieved, what should and what should not be attempted. They and they alone hold the key to secular success as well as to spiritual salvation. Omniscience belongs only to God. But only by immersing ourselves in His Word—His theological or metaphysical principles, embodied at their lowest in instincts and ancient superstititions which are but primitive ways, tested by time, of divining and obeying His laws—whereas reasoning is an effort to substitute one's own arbitrary rules—dare we hope for wisdom. Practical wisdom is to a large degree knowledge of the inevitable: of what, given our world order, could not but happen; and conversely, of how things cannot be, or could not have been, done; of why some schemes must, cannot help but, end in failure, although for this no demonstrative or scientific reason can be given. The rare capacity for seeing this we rightly call a 'sense of reality'—it is a sense of what fits with what, of what cannot exist with what; and it goes by many names: insight, wisdom, practical genius, a sense of the past, an understanding of life and of human character.

Tolstoy's view is not very different; save that he gives as the reason for the folly of our exaggerated claims to understand or determine events not foolish or blasphemous efforts to do without special, i.e. supernatural knowledge, but our ignorance of too many among the vast number of interrelations—the minute determining causes of events; if we began to

[64]

know the causal network in its infinite variety, we should cease to praise and blame, boast and regret, or look on human beings as heroes or villains, but should submit with due humility to unavoidable necessity. Yet to say no more than this is to give a travesty of his beliefs. It is indeed Tolstoy's explicit doctrine in *War and Peace* that all truth is in science—in the knowledge of material causes—and that we consequently render ourselves ridiculous by arriving at conclusions on too little evidence, comparing in this regard unfavourably with peasants or savages who, being not so very much more ignorant, at least make more modest claims; but this is not the view of the world that, in fact, underlies either *War and Peace* or *Anna Karenina* or any other work which belongs to this period of Tolstoy's life. Kutuzov is wise and not merely clever as, for example, the time-serving Drubetzkoy or Bilibin are clever, and he is not a victim to abstract theories or dogma as the German military experts are; he is unlike them, and is wiser than they—but this is so not because he knows more facts than they and has at his finger tips a greater number of the 'minute causes' of events than his advisers or his adversaries—than Pfuel or Paulucci or Berthier or the King of Naples. Karataev brings light to Pierre, whereas the Freemasons did not, but this is so not because he happens to have scientific information superior to that possessed by the Moscow lodges; Levin goes through an experience during his work in the fields, and Prince Andrey while lying wounded on the battlefield of Austerlitz, but in neither case has there been a discovery of fresh facts or of new laws in any ordinary sense. On the contrary the greater one's accumulation of facts, the more futile one's activity, the more hopeless one's failure—as shown by the group of reformers who surround Alexander. They and men like them are only saved from Faustian despair by stupidity (like the Germans and the military experts and experts generally) or by vanity (like Napoleon) or by frivolity (like Oblonsky) or by heartlessness (like Karenin). What is it that Pierre, Prince Andrey, Levin discover? and what are they searching for, and what is the centre and climax of the spiritual crisis resolved by the experience that transforms their lives? Not the chastening realization of how little of the totality of facts and laws known to Laplace's omniscient observer, they—Pierre, Levin, etc.—can claim to have discovered; not a simple admission of Socratic ignorance. Still less does it consist in what is almost at the opposite pole—in a new, a more precise awareness of the 'iron laws' that govern our lives, in a vision of nature as a machine or a factory, in the cosmology of the great materialists, Diderot or Lamettrie or Doctor Cabanis, or of the mid-nineteenth scientific writers idolized by the 'nihilist' Bazarov in Turgenev's *Fathers and Children*; nor yet in some transcendent sense of the inexpressible one-ness of life to which poets, mystics and metaphysicians have in all ages testified. Nevertheless, something *is* perceived; there is a vision, or at least a glimpse, a moment of revelation which in some sense explains and reconciles, a theodicy, a justification of what exists and happens, as well as its elucidation. What does it consist in? Tolstoy does not tell us in so many words: for when (in his later, explicitly didactic works) he sets out to do so, his doctrine is no longer the same. Yet no reader of *War and Peace* can be wholly unaware of what he is being told. And that not only in the Kutuzov, or Karataev scenes or other quasi-theological or quasi-metaphysical passages— but even more, for example, in the narrative, nonphilosophical section of the epilogue, in which Pierre, Natasha, Nikolai Rostov, Princess Marie, are shown anchored in their new solid, sober lives with their established day to day routine. We are here plainly

[66]

intended to see that these 'heroes' of the novel—the 'good' people—have now, after the storms and agonies of ten years and more, achieved a kind of peace, based on some degree of understanding; understanding of what? of the need to submit; to what? not simply to the will of God (not, at any rate during the writing of the great novels, in the eighteen sixties or seventies) nor to the 'iron laws' of the sciences; but to the permanent relationships of things,[1] and the universal texture of human life, wherein alone truth and justice are to be found by a kind of 'natural'—somewhat Aristotelian—knowledge. To do this is, above all, to grasp what human will and human reason can do, and what they cannot. How can this be known? not by a specific inquiry and discovery, but by an awareness, not necessarily explicit or conscious, of certain general characteristics of human life and experience. And the most important and most pervasive of these is the crucial line that divides the 'surface' from the 'depths'—on the one hand the world of perceptible, describable, analysable data, both physical and psychological, both 'external' and 'inner', both public and private, with which the sciences can deal, although they have in some regions —those outside physics—made so little progress; and, on the other hand, the order which, as it were, 'contains' and determines the structure of experience, the framework in which it—that is, we and all that we experience—must be conceived as being set, that which enters into our habits of thought, action, feeling, our emotions, hopes, wishes, our ways of talking, believing, reacting, being. We—sentient creatures— are in part living in a world the constituents of which we can discover, classify and act upon by rational, scientific, deliberately planned methods; but in part

[1] Almost in the sense in which this phrase is used by Montesquieu in the opening sentence of *L'Esprit des Lois*.

(Tolstoy and Maistre, and many thinkers with them, say much the larger part) we are immersed and submerged in a medium that, precisely to the degree to which we inevitably take it for granted as part of ourselves, we do not and cannot observe as if from the outside; cannot identify, measure and seek to manipulate; cannot even be wholly aware of, inasmuch as it enters too intimately into all our experience, is itself too closely interwoven with all that we are and do to be lifted out of the flow (it *is* the flow) and observed with scientific detachment, as an object. It—the medium in which we are—determines our most permanent categories, our standards of truth and falsehood, of reality and appearance, of the good and the bad, of the central and the peripheral, the subjective and the objective, of the beautiful and the ugly, of movement and rest, of past, present and future, of one and many; hence neither these, nor any other explicitly conceived categories or concepts can be applied to it—for it is itself but a vague name for the totality that includes these categories, these concepts, the ultimate framework, the basic presuppositions wherewith we function. Nevertheless though we cannot analyse the medium without some (impossible) vantage point outside it (for there is no 'outside') yet some human beings are better aware—although they cannot describe it—of the texture and direction of these 'submerged' portions of their own and everyone else's lives; better aware of this than others, who either ignore the existence of the all-pervasive medium (the 'flow of life'), and are rightly called superficial; or else try to apply to it instruments—scientific, metaphysical, etc., adapted solely to objects above the surface, i.e. the relatively conscious, manipulable portion of our experience, and so achieve absurdities in their theories and humiliating failures in practice. Wisdom is ability to allow for the (at

[68]

least by us) unalterable medium in which we act—as we allow for the pervasiveness, say, of time or space which characterize all our experience; and to discount, less or more consciously, the 'inevitable trends', the 'imponderables', the 'way things are going'. It is not scientific knowledge, but a special sensitiveness to the contours of the circumstances in which we happen to be placed; it is a capacity for living without falling foul of some permanent condition or factor which cannot be either altered, or even fully described or calculated; an ability to be guided by rules of thumb —the 'immemorial wisdom' said to reside in peasants and other 'simple folk'—where rules of science do not, in principle, apply. This inexpressible sense of cosmic orientation is the 'sense of reality', 'the knowledge' of how to live. Sometimes Tolstoy does speak as if science could in principle, if not in practice, penetrate and conquer everything; and if it did, then we should know the causes of all there is, and know we were not free, but wholly determined—which is all that the wisest can ever know. So, too, Maistre talks as if the schoolmen knew more than we, through their superior techniques: but what they knew was still, in some sense, 'the facts': the subject-matter of the sciences; St. Thomas knew incomparably more than Newton, and with more precision and more certainty, but what he knew was of the same kind. But despite this lip-service to the truth-finding capacities of natural science or theology, these avowals remain purely formal: and a very different belief finds expression in the positive doctrines of both Maistre and Tolstoy. Aquinas is praised by Maistre not for being a better mathematician than d'Alembert or Monge; Kutuzov's virtue does not, according to Tolstoy, consist in his being a better, more scientific theorist of war than Pfuel or Paulucci. These great men are wiser, not more know-ledgeable; it is not their deductive or inductive

[69]

reasoning that makes them masters; their vision is 'profounder', they see something the others fail to see; they see the way the world goes, what goes with what, and what never will be brought together; they see what can be and what cannot; how men live and to what ends, what they do and suffer, and how and why they act, and should act, thus and not otherwise. This 'seeing' purveys, in a sense, no fresh information about the universe; it is an awareness of the interplay of the imponderable with the ponderable, of the 'shape' of things in general or of a specific situation, or of a particular character, which is precisely what cannot be deduced from, or even formulated in terms of, the laws of nature demanded by scientific determinism. Whatever can be subsumed under such laws scientists can and do deal with; that needs no 'wisdom'; and to deny science its rights because of the existence of this superior 'wisdom', is a wanton invasion of scientific territory, and a confusion of categories. Tolstoy, at least, does not go to the length of denying the efficacy of physics in its own sphere; but he thinks this sphere trivial in comparison with what is permanently out of the reach of science—the social, moral, political, spiritual worlds, which cannot be sorted out and described and predicted by any science, because the proportion in them of 'submerged', uninspectable life is too high. The insight that reveals the nature and structure of these worlds is not a mere makeshift substitute, an empirical *pis aller* to which recourse is had only so long as the relevant scientific techniques are insufficiently refined; its business is altogether different: it does what no science can claim to do; it distinguishes the real from the sham, the worthwhile from the worthless, that which can be done or borne from what cannot be; and does so without giving rational grounds for its pronouncements, if only because 'rational' and 'irrational' are terms that

[70]

themselves acquire their meanings and uses in relation to—'by growing out of'—it, and not *vice versa*. For what are the data of such understanding if not the ultimate soil, the framework, the atmosphere, the context, the medium (to use whatever metaphor is most expressive) in which all our thoughts and acts are felt, valued, judged, in the inevitable ways that they are? It is the ever present sense of this framework—of this movement of events, or changing pattern of characteristics —as something 'inexorable', universal, pervasive, not alterable by us, not in our power, in the sense of power in which the progress of scientific knowledge has given us power over nature, that is at the root of Tolstoy's determinism, and of his realism, pessimism, and of his (and Maistre's) contempt for the faith placed in reason alike of science and of worldly common sense. It is 'there'—the framework, the foundation of everything, and the wise man alone has a sense of it; Pierre gropes for it; Kutuzov feels it in his bones; Karataev is at one with it. All Tolstoy's heroes attain to at least intermittent glimpses of it—and this it is that makes all the conventional explanations, the scientific, the historical, those of unreflective 'good sense', seem so hollow and, at their most pretentious, so shamefully false. Tolstoy, himself, too, knows that the truth is there, and not 'here'—not in the regions susceptible to observation, discrimination, constructive imagination, not in the power of microscopic perception and analysis of which he is so much the greatest master of our time; but he has not, himself, seen it face to face; for he has not, do what he might, a vision of the whole; he is not, he is remote from being, a hedgehog; and what he sees is not the one, but, always with an ever growing minuteness, in all its teeming individuality, with an obsessive, inescapable, incorruptible, all penetrating lucidity which maddens him, the many.

VII

We are part of a larger scheme of things than we can
understand. We cannot describe it in the way in
which external objects or the characters of other
people can be described, by isolating them somewhat
from the historical 'flow' in which they have their
being, and from the 'submerged', unfathomed, portions of themselves to which professional historians
have, according to Tolstoy, paid so little heed; for we
ourselves live in this whole and by it, and are wise only
in the measure to which we make our peace with it.
For until and unless we do so (only after much bitter
suffering, if we are to trust Aeschylus and the Book of
Job, we shall protest and suffer in vain, and make
sorry fools of ourselves (as Napoleon did) into the
bargain. This sense of the circumambient stream,
defiance of whose nature through stupidity or over-
weening egotism will make our acts and thoughts self-
defeating, is the vision of the unity of experience, the
sense of history, the true knowledge of reality, the
belief in the incommunicable wisdom of the sage (or
the saint) which, *mutatis mutandis*, is common to
Tolstoy and Maistre. Their realism is of a similar sort:
the natural enemy of romanticism, sentimentalism and
'historicism' as much as of aggressive 'scientism'.
Their purpose is not to distinguish the little that is
known or done from the limitless ocean of what, in
principle, could or one day would be known or done,
whether by advance in the knowledge of the natural
sciences or of metaphysics or of the historical sciences,
or by a return to the past, or by some other method;
what they seek to establish are the eternal frontiers of
our knowledge and power, to demarcate them from
what cannot in principle ever be known or altered by
men. According to Maistre our destiny lies in original
sin—in the fact that we are human—finite, fallible,
vicious, vain and that all our empirical knowledge

(as opposed to the teachings of the Church) is infected by error and monomania. According to Tolstoy all our knowledge is necessarily empirical—there is no other—but it will never conduct us to true understanding, but only to an accumulation of arbitrarily abstracted bits and pieces of information; yet that seems to him (as much as to any metaphysician of the Idealist school which he despised) worthless beside, and unintelligible save in so far as it derives from and points to this inexpressible but very palpable kind of superior understanding which alone is worth pursuing. Sometimes Tolstoy comes near to saying what it is: the more we know, he tells us, about a given human action, the more inevitable, determined it seems to us to be; why? because the more we know about all the relevant conditions and antecedents, the more difficult we find it to think away various circumstances, and conjecture what might have occurred without them—and as we go on removing in our imagination what we know to be true, fact by fact, this becomes not merely difficult but impossible. Tolstoy's meaning is not obscure. We are what we are, and live in a given situation which has the characteristics—physical, psychological, social, etc.—that it has; what we think, feel, do, is conditioned by it, including our capacity for conceiving possible alternatives, whether in the present or future or past. Our imagination and ability to calculate, our power of conceiving, let us say, what might have been, if the past had, in this or that particular, been otherwise, soon reaches its natural limits —limits created both by the weakness of our capacity for calculating alternatives—'might have beens'—and (we may add by a logical extension of Tolstoy's argument) even more by the fact that our thoughts, the terms in which they occur, the symbols themselves, are what they are, are themselves determined by the actual structure of our world. Our images and powers of

[73]

conception are limited by the fact that our world possesses certain characteristics and not others: a world too different is (empirically) not conceivable at all: some minds are more imaginative than others, but all stop somewhere. The world is a system and a network: to conceive of men as 'free' is to think of them as capable of having, at some past juncture, acted in some fashion other than that in which they did act; it is to think of what consequences would have come of such unfulfilled possibilities and in what respects the world would have been different, as a result, from the world as it now is. It is difficult enough to do this in the case of artificial, purely deductive systems, as, for example in chess, where the permutations are finite in number, and clear in type—having been arranged so by us, artificially—so that the combinations are calculable. But if you apply this method to the vague, rich texture of the real world, and try to work out the implications of this or that unrealized plan or unperformed action —the effect of it on the totality of later events—basing yourself on such knowledge of causal laws, probabilities, etc., as you have, you will find that the greater the number of 'minute' causes you discriminate, the more appalling becomes the task of 'deducing' any consequence of the 'unhinging' of each of these, one by one; for each of the consequences affects the whole of the rest of the uncountable totality of events and things; which unlike chess is not defined in terms of a finite, arbitrarily chosen set of concepts and rules. And if, whether in real life or even in chess, you begin to tamper with basic notions—continuity of space, divisibility of time and the like, you will soon reach a stage in which the symbols fail to function, your thoughts become confused and paralysed. Consequently the fuller our knowledge of facts and of their connections the more difficult to conceive alternatives; the clearer and more exact the terms—or the categories—in

[74]

which we conceive and describe the world, the more
fixed our world structure, the less 'free' acts seem. To
know these limits, both of imagination and, ultimately,
of thought itself, is to come face to face with the
'inexorable' unifying pattern of the world; to realize
our identity with it, to submit to it, is to find truth and
peace. This is not mere Oriental fatalism, nor the
mechanistic determinism of the celebrated German
materialists of the day, Professors Büchner and Vogt,
or Dr. Moleschott, admired so deeply by the revolutionary 'nihilists' of Tolstoy's generation in Russia;
nor is it a yearning for mystical illumination or integration. It is scrupulously empirical, rational, tough-
minded and realistic. But its emotional cause is a
passionate desire for a monistic vision of life on the
part of a fox bitterly intent upon seeing in the manner
of a hedgehog.

This is remarkably close to Maistre's dogmatic
affirmations: we must achieve an attitude of assent to
the demands of history which are the voice of God
speaking through His servants and His divine institutions, not made by human hands and not destruc-
tible by them. We must attune ourselves to the true
word of God, the inner 'go' of things; but what it is in
concrete cases, how we are to conduct our private
lives or public policies—of that we are told little by
either critic of optimistic liberalism. Nor can we
expect to be told. For the positive vision escapes them.
Tolstoy's language—and Maistre's no less—is adapted
to the opposite activity. It is in analysing, identifying
sharply, marking differences, isolating concrete examples, piercing to the heart of each individual entity
per se, that Tolstoy rises to the full height of his
genius; and similarly Maistre achieves his brilliant
effects by pinning down and offering for public
pillory—by a *montage sur l'épingle*—the absurdities
committed by his opponents. They are acute observers

of the varieties of experience: every attempt to represent these falsely, or to offer delusive explanations of them, they detect immediately and deride savagely. Yet they both know that the full truth—the ultimate basis of the correlation of all the ingredients of the universe with one another—the context in which alone, anything that they, or anyone else, can say can ever be true or false, trivial or important—that resides in a synoptic vision which, because they do not possess it, they cannot express. What is it that Pierre has learnt, of which Princess Marie's marriage is an acceptance, that Prince Andrey all his life pursued with such agony? Like Augustine, Tolstoy can only say what it is not. His genius is devastatingly destructive. He can only attempt to point towards his goal by exposing the false signposts to it; to isolate the truth by annihilating that which it is not—namely all that can be said in the clear, analytical language that corresponds to the all too clear, but necessarily limited, vision of the foxes. Like Moses, he must halt at the borders of the Promised Land; without it his journey is meaningless; but he cannot enter it; yet he knows that it exists, and can tell us, as no one else has ever told us, all that it is not—above all, not anything that art, or science or civilization or rational criticism can achieve. And so too Joseph de Maistre. He is the Voltaire of reaction. Every new doctrine since the ages of faith is torn to shreds with ferocious skill and malice. The pretenders are exposed and struck down one by one; the armoury of weapons against liberal and humanitarian doctrines is the most effective ever assembled. But the throne remains vacant, the positive doctrine is too unconvincing. Maistre sighs for the Dark Ages, but no sooner are plans for the undoing of the French Revolution—a return to the *status quo ante*—suggested by his fellow *émigrés*, than he denounces them as childish nonsense—an attempt to behave as if what has occurred and changed us all irretrievably, had never been. To try to reverse the Revolution, he wrote, was as if one had been invited to drain the Lake of Geneva by bottling its waters in a wine cellar.

There is no kinship between him and those who really did believe in the possibility of some kind of return—neo-medievalists from Wackenroder and Görres and Cobbett to the late Mr. Chesterton and Slavophils and Distributists and pre-Raphaelites and other nostalgic romantics; for he believed, as Tolstoy also did, in the exact opposite: in the 'inexorable' power of the present moment: in our inability to do away with the sum of conditions which cumulatively determine our basic categories, an order which we can never fully describe or, otherwise than by some immediate awareness of them, come to know.

The quarrel between these rival types of knowledge—that which results from methodical inquiry, and the more impalpable kind that consists in the 'sense of reality', in 'wisdom'—is very old. And the claims of both have generally been recognized to have some validity: the bitterest clashes have been concerned with the precise line which marks the frontier between their territories. Those who made large claims for non-scientific knowledge have been accused by their adversaries of irrationalism and obscurantism, of the deliberate rejection, in favour of the emotions or blind prejudice, of reliable public standards of ascertainable truth; and have, in their turn, charged their opponents, the ambitious champions of science, with making absurd claims, promising the impossible, issuing false prospectuses, of undertaking to explain history or the arts or the states of the individual soul (and to change them too) when quite plainly they do not begin to understand what they are; when the results of their labours, even when they are not nugatory, tend to take unpredicted, often catastrophic directions—and all this because they will not, being vain and headstrong, admit that too many factors in too many situations are always unknown, and not discoverable by the methods of natural science. Better, surely, not to pretend to calculate the incalculable, not to pretend that there is an Archimedean point outside the world whence everything is measurable and alterable; better to use in each context the methods that seem to fit it best, that give the (pragmatically) best results; to resist the temptations of Procrustes; above all to distinguish what is isolable, classifiable and capable of objective study and sometimes of precise measurement and manipulation, from the most permanent, ubiquitous, inescapable, intimately present features of our world, which, if anything, are over-familiar, so that their 'inexorable' pressure, being too much with us, is scarcely felt, hardly noticed, and cannot conceivably be observed in perspective, be an object of study. This is the distinction that permeates the thought of Pascal and Blake, Rousseau and Schelling, Goethe and Coleridge, Chateaubriand and Carlyle; of all those who speak of the reasons of the heart, or of men's moral or spiritual nature, of sublimity and depth, of the 'profounder' insight of poets and prophets, of special kinds of understanding, of inwardly comprehending, or being at one with, the world. To these latter thinkers both Tolstoy and Maistre belong. Tolstoy blames everything on our ignorance of empirical causes, and Maistre on the abandonment of Thomist logic or the theology of the Catholic Church. But these avowed professions are belied by the tone and content of what in fact the two great critics say. Both stress, over and over again, the contrast between the 'inner' and the 'outer', the 'surface' which alone is lighted by the rays of science and of reason, and the 'depths'—'the real life lived by men'. For Maistre, as later for Barrès, true knowledge—wisdom—lies in an understanding of, and communion with, *la terre et les morts* (what has this to do with Thomist logic?)—the great unalterable movement created by the links between the dead and the living and the yet unborn and the land on which they live; and it is this, perhaps, or something akin to it, that in their respective fashions, Burke and Taine, and their many imitators have attempted to convey. As for Tolstoy, to him such mystical conservatism was peculiarly detestable, since it seemed to him to evade the central question by merely restating it, concealed in a cloud of pompous rhetoric, as the answer. Yet he, too, in the end, presents us with the vision, dimly discerned by Kutuzov and by Pierre, of Russia in her vastness, and what she could and what she could not do or suffer, and how and when—all of which Napoleon and his advisers (who knew a great deal but not of what was relevant to the issue) did not perceive; and so (although their knowledge of history and science and minute causes was perhaps greater than Kutuzov's or Pierre's) were led duly to their doom. Maistre's paeans to the superior science of the great Christian soldiers of the past and Tolstoy's lamentations about our scientific ignorance should not mislead anyone to the nature of what they are in fact defending: awareness of the 'deep currents', the *raisons de cœur*, which they did not indeed themselves know by direct experience; but beside which, they were convinced, the devices of science were but a snare and a delusion.

Despite their deep dissimilarity and indeed violent opposition to one another, Tolstoy's sceptical realism and Maistre's dogmatic authoritarianism are blood brothers. For both spring from an agonized belief in a single, serene vision, in which all problems are resolved, all doubts stilled, peace and understanding finally achieved. Deprived of this vision, they devoted all their formidable resources from their very different, and indeed often incompatible, positions, to the elimination of all possible adversaries and critics of it. The faiths for whose mere abstract possibility they fought were not, indeed, identical. It is the predicament in which they found themselves and that caused them to dedicate their strength to the lifelong task of destruction, it is their common enemies and the strong likeness between their temperaments that make them odd but unmistakable allies in a war which they were both conscious of fighting until their dying day.

VIII

Opposed as Tolstoy and Maistre were—one the apostle of the gospel that all men are brothers, the other the cold defender of the claims of violence, blind sacrifice, and eternal suffering—they were united by inability to escape from the same tragic paradox: they were both by nature sharp-eyed foxes, inescapably aware of sheer, *de facto* differences which divide and forces which disrupt the human world, observers utterly incapable of being deceived by the many subtle devices, the unifying systems and faiths and sciences, by which the superficial or the desperate sought to conceal the chaos from themselves and from one another. Both looked for a harmonious universe, but everywhere found war and disorder, which no attempt to cheat, however heavily disguised, could even begin to hide; and so, in a condition of final despair, offered to throw away the terrible weapons of criticism, with which both, but particularly Tolstoy, were overgenerously endowed, in favour of the single great vision, something too indivisibly simple and remote from normal intellectual processes to be assailable by the instruments of reason, and therefore, perhaps, offering a path to peace and salvation. Maistre began as a moderate liberal and ended by pulverizing the new nineteenth-century world from the solitary citadel of his own variety of ultramontane Catholicism. Tolstoy began with a view of human life and history which contradicted all his knowledge, all his gifts, all his inclinations, and which, in consequence, he could scarcely be said to have embraced in the sense of practising it, either as a writer or as a man. From this, in his old age, he passed into a form of life in which he tried to resolve the glaring contradiction between what he believed about men and events, and what he thought he believed, or ought to believe, by behaving, in the end, as if factual questions of this kind were not the fundamental issues at all, only the trivial preoccupations of an idle, ill-conducted life, while the real questions were quite different. But it was of no use: the Muse cannot be cheated. Tolstoy was the least superficial of men: he could not swim with the tide without being drawn irresistibly beneath the surface to investigate the darker depths below; and he could not avoid seeing what he saw and doubting even that; he could close his eyes but not forget that he was doing so; his appalling, destructive, sense of what was false frustrated this final effort at self-deception as it did all the earlier ones; and he died in agony, oppressed by the burden of his intellectual infallibility and his sense of perpetual moral error, the greatest of those who can neither reconcile, nor leave unreconciled, the conflict of what there is with what there ought to be. Tolstoy's sense of reality was until the end too devastating to be compatible with any moral ideal which he was able to construct out of the fragments into which his intellect shivered the world, and he dedicated all of his vast strength of mind and will to the lifelong denial of this fact. At once insanely proud and filled with self-hatred, omniscient and doubting everything, cold and violently passionate, contemptuous and self-abasing, tormented and detached, surrounded by an adoring family, by devoted followers, by the admiration of the entire civilized world, and yet almost wholly isolated, he is the most tragic of the great writers, a desperate old man, beyond human aid, wandering self-blinded at Colonus.

INDEX OF PROPER NAMES

Aeschylus, 72
Akhsharumov, N., 7, 32, 38
Alembert, J. L. d', 69
Alexander I, Tsar, 17, 22, 24, 28, 57, 61, 65
Andrey, Prince (Bolkonsky), 16, 54, 65, 66, 76
Anna Karenina, 36, 65
Annenkov, Pavel, 5
Annunzio, G. d', 49
Antaeus, 5
Apostolov, N., 12n., 13n.
Aquinas, Thomas (Saint), 69
Archilochus, 1
Aristotle, 2
Augustine (Saint), 76
Austerlitz, Battle of, 16, 54, 65
Austria, 22

Bagration, Prince P., 16
Balzac, H. de, 2
Barrès, M., 78
Bartenev, P., 48
Bazarov, 66
Beaumarchais, P. de, 24
Belinsky, V., 6
Bennett, Arnold, 20
Bennigsen, General L., 18
Bergson, Henri, 31
Berthier, Marshal A., 65
Bezukhov, Hélène, see Hélène
Bezukhov, Pierre, see Pierre
Bilibin, 65
Biryukov, P. I, 5n., 7, 55n.
Blake, W., 78
Blok, A., 3
Bogoslavsky, E., 5n
Bolkonsky, Prince, 51
Bolkonsky, Prince Andrey, see Andrey, Prince
Bolkonsky, Princess Marie, see Marie, Princess
Borodino, Battle of, 16, 18, 25

Botkin, V., 6, 9
Boyer, P., 47, 47n.
Büchner, L., 75
Buckle, H. T., 29, 44
Burke, E., 31, 79

Cabanis, P. J., 66
Cagliari, 55
Carlyle, T., 78
Catherine II, Empress, 12
Chartreuse de Parme, La, 18n., 47
Chateaubriand, Vicomte F. R. de, 78
Chekhov, A., 3
Chernyshevsky, N., 44
Chertkov, V., 12n.
Coleridge, S. T., 78
Colonus, 82
Comte, A., 14, 44
Contrat Social, 24, 43
Correspondance Diplomatique, 50
Cossacks, The, 4n.
Culture Française en Russie, La, 55n.
Curiatii, 51

D'Alembert, J. L., see Alembert, J. L. d'
Danilevsky, 7
D'Annunzio, G., see Annunzio, G. d'
Dante, 2, 3
Darwin, C., 14
De Maistre, J., see Maistre, J. de
De Maupassant, G., see Maupassant, G. de
D'Enghien, Duc L., see Enghien, Duc L. d'
Dickens, C., 12
Diderot, D., 24, 42, 66
Dostoevsky, F., 2, 3, 41, 44, 60n.

Drissa, 18, 50
Drubetzkoy, Prince B., 65

Émile, 43
Encyclopaedists, The French, 44, 58
Enghien, Duc L. d', 51
England, 20
Erasmus, D., 2
Europe, 23
Eykhenbaum, B., 8n., 36, 36n., 42n., 48n., 59n.

Fabrice (Del Dongo), 47
Fathers and Children, 66
Fet, A., 6, 9
Fili, 28
Flaubert, G., 5, 20
France, 20, 21, 22, 23, 42, 49
Frederick II, King, 54

Geneva, lake of, 77
Georges, Mlle, 51
Germany, 42, 58
Gibbon, E., 29
Gide, A., 20
Goethe, J. W., 2, 78
Gogol', N., 3
Gorky, M., 6on.
Görres, L., 77
Guerre et la Paix, La, 46, 59
Gusev, N. N., 13, 13n.

Haumant, E., 8n., 55n.
Hegel, G. W. F., 2, 11, 45
Hélène (Bezukhov), 50, 61
Herodotus, 2
Horatius, 51
Hume, D., 12
Huns, The, 13

Ibsen, H., 2
Igor, Prince, 13
Ilyin, Prof., 7n.
Italy, 22
Ivan IV, Tsar, 13, 24

Ivanov, Prof., 13

Job, 72
Jourdain, Monsieur, 11
Joyce, J., 2

Karataev, P., 28, 46, 65, 66, 71
Karenin, 66
Karenina, Anna, see *Anna Karenina*
Kareyev, N., 8n., 32, 32n., 33, 34, 35, 38
Kautsky, K., 8n.
Koltovskaya, A., 13
Kuragin, Prince Vassili, see Vassili, Prince
Kurbsky, Prince, 24
Kutuzov, Field Marshal M., 28, 32, 50, 65, 66, 69, 71, 79

Lamennais, F. de, 60
Lamettrie, J. O. de, 66
Laplace, P., Count, 26, 66
Lenin, V. I., 8n.
Leon, D., 7
Leontyev, K. N., 7
Levin, 36, 65, 66
Louis XIV, King, 21
Louis XVIII, King, 22
Lubbock, P., 7
Lucretius, 2

Maistre, J. de, 48, 49, 50, 51, 52, 53n., 54, 55, 56, 57, 58, 59, 59n., 60, 6on., 61, 62, 63, 68, 69, 71, 72, 75, 76, 78, 79, 80
Maistre, R. de, 50
Marie, Princess (Bolkonsky), 66, 76
Marx, K., 14, 27
Maude, A., 7
Maupassant, G. de, 21n.
Merezhkovsky, D., 7
Mill, J. S., 44
Moleschott, J., 75

Molière, J. B., 2
Monge, G., 69
Montaigne, M. de, 2
Montesquieu, Baron C. de S.
de, 12, 67n.
Moscow, 17, 22
Moses, 76

Napoleon I, Emperor, 19, 22,
23, 24, 28, 34, 49, 51, 54, 66,
72, 79
Natasha (Rostov), 66
Navalikhin, C., 6n.
Nazar'ev, V. N., 13, 13n.
Newton, I., 69
Nicholas I, Tsar, 56
Nietzsche, F., 49
Norov, A. S., 6n.

Oblonsky, Prince S., 66
Obninsky, V. P., 8n., 28n.
Oleg, Prince, 13
Omodeo, A., 48n.

Paris, 22
Pascal, B., 2, 78
Paulucci, Marchese, 18, 50, 65,
69
Pertsev, V., 8n.
Pfuel, General E., 18, 65, 69
Pisarev, D., 44
Plato, 2
Pobyedonostsev, K., 61
Pogodin, M., 43
Pokrovsky, K., 28n., 55n.
Polner, T., 8n., 28n.
Poulet, M. de, 9n.
Procrustes, 78
Proudhon, P.-J., 46, 59, 59n.
Proust, M., 2
Pushkin, A., 2, 3
Pyatkovsky, A., 6n.

Rostov, Natasha, see Natasha
Rostov, Nikolai, 16, 66

Rousseau, J. J., 12, 25, 42, 43,
47, 62, 78
Rousseauism, 46
Rubinshteyn, M., 8n., 25n.
Russia, 17, 22, 49, 58, 61, 79

Saint Helena, island of, 23
Saint Petersburg, 49, 51, 61
Saint-Simon, H. de, 14
Samarin, Yv., 43
Sardinia, 49
Schelling, F. W. J. von, 45, 78
Scherer, A., Mme, 50, 51
Schöngraben, battle of, 16
Schopenhauer, A., 47
Sebastopol Stories, The, 4n.
Shakespeare, W., 2, 3
Shaw, G. B., 20, 21n.
Shelgunov, N. V., 6
Shklovsky, V., 6n., 28n., 42n.
Simmons, Prof. E., 7
Soirées de St. Pétersbourg, Les,
50, 53n., 54n.
Sorel, A., 8n., 9, 55, 55n., 60
Spencer, H., 44
Speransky, M., 17, 57
Spinoza, B., 27
Staël, Mme de, 24
Stalin, J. V., 8n.
Stein, Baron von, 22, 24
Stendhal, 18n., 47, 48, 54, 60
Sterne, L., 12
Stroganov, Count G., 51

Taine, H., 79
Talleyrand, Prince de C. M.,
22
Temryuk, King, 13
Thiers, L. A., 12
Tolstoy, Count L. N., *passim*
Tolstoy, N., 48
Turgenev, I. S., 3, 5, 20, 40, 66
Tyutchev, F., 6, 44

Vassili, Prince (Kuragin), 50

Vienna, 23
Vittmer, A., 6n.
Vogt, K., 75
Vogüé, E. M. de, 1, 7, 9, 60
Voltaire, 62, 63, 76
Vyazemsky, Prince P., 9

Wackenroder, W. H., 77
War and Peace, 4n., 5, 6, 7, 9,
    14, 14n., 15, 16, 21, 21n.,
    27n., 28, 29, 30, 31n., 32, 33,
    38, 40, 42, 44, 46, 48, 51,
    59n., 61, 65, 66

Waterloo, 47
Wells, H. G., 20
Woolf, Virginia, 19

Yakovenko, Prof., 7n.
Yasnaya Polyana, 50

Zen'kovsky, Prof. S., 7n.
Zhikharev, S. P., 51, 51n.
Zweig, S., 7